A Short History of American Catholicism

A Short History of American Catholicism

Martin E. Marty

ThomasMore

A DIVISION OF TABOR PUBLISHING

Allen, Texas

Send all inquiries to:
Thomas More Publishing
200 East Bethany Drive
Allen, Texas 75002–3804

Printed in the United States of America

ISBN 0–88347–320–8

1 2 3 4 5   99 98 97 96 95

To Sister Candida Lund
with affection
thirty years after she invited me
to take part in making
American Catholic history

Contents

A Church Becoming a People, But Also Remaining a Church

This book has a prosaic title: *A Short History of American Catholicism*. An earlier version was called *An Invitation to American Catholic History*, but ten years after readers were originally invited, it became time to be more clear about what we are doing between these book covers. Nothing could be more clear than the title.

It parallels the title of my first book, *A Short History of Christianity*. Almost four decades ago a Jewish publisher and his Protestant editor took me for a long evening walk in St. Louis and asked me, fresh from doctoral work and untried as an author, to write a book with that name. In 1959 it appeared, one that has stayed in print ever since and is probably my best-seller. So I am invoking "the luck of the Irish" or of any other Catholic ethnic group, or the luck of the Jew, or the Protestant, since they inspired the first title, and launch this volume with the hope that it will long be in print and be a good-seller, of service to many readers. The title, I said, is clear, but we still need to point to its four main words in order to help make sure that we are clear about our purposes and topic.

First, the book is *short*. Busy readers can gain a grasp of the outlines and profiles of American Catholicism through five centuries, after which the curious whose appetites have been whetted can pursue details and other interpretations in long books from longer shelves in large libraries. As books go, yes, this is short; no one need argue about that first word.

A *history* it is, purely and simply, though scholars might argue about what history, or *a* history is. This one qualifies as a narrative, a story, about the past, inspired by our contemporary curiosities. All story-telling is selective. By choosing to talk about Catholics instead of Quakers and Americans instead of Nigerians, I am ruling out many good topics while accenting what is important about the chosen one.

The third word, *American*, invites a bit of controversy, since it is not really about every place that is or can be called American. There is only bare mention of Latin, or South, or Central America, and Canada is slighted in this story of the United States. The title is not misleading; citizens of the United States habitually and instinctively monopolize the word and will likely continue to do so. It is somewhat presumptuous; but "United States" does not make a good adjective; *A Short History of United Statesian Catholicism* does not work, and *A Short History of Catholicism in the United States* gets long and springs the rhythm. And "History" and "United States" have already been used in connections of the American story, so the zone is getting crowded. We ask our Canadian neighbors and those sensitive to nuances to beg our pardon as they must beg almost 250 million pardons for what almost 250 million United Statesians tend to do every day.

The fourth word, *Catholicism*, also deserves some scrutiny and may demand some defense. The earlier book had the word *Christianity*, not *The Christian Church* in its title. There is some difference between the two. The Church, the body of Christ, is a set of people, a "thing," something with (fortunately hard to find and define) boundaries, a living pulse. Christianity is both the Church and the culture it creates or that helps shape it; Christianity is a people and a set of signals, symbols, artifacts, legacies that would no doubt survive long after the Church would die, if the Church of Jesus Christ *could* die. Catholicism as opposed to the Catholic *Church* in a title allows us to tell the story of a people and the artifacts and influences of the surrounding culture without being so very worried about defining the Church as such.

Most authors who love to play with words no doubt nurture the hope that some day something they say or write will inspire lexicographers to sneak one of their words into the dictionary. My first choice would be the word "descript." The dictionary now has the term "nondescript," meaning "neither here nor there," characterless. Something that is "descript" is "either here or there," full of character. This book is an attempt to describe a descript people, institution, way of life, and set of ideas and productions. Its author recognizes that, for all the variety in the world five centuries ago, much of Catholicism looked and was more descript and easily describable than it is today. Some readers of the last two chapters will even wonder whether Catholicism is becoming or has become nondescript, so urgent does this story suggest the quest for descriptness has become.

How to pose the issue? One day over lunch my University of Chicago colleague Father Andrew Greeley and I were talking about two trends among major American religious bodies. On one hand, there were the Mormons, also called The Church of Jesus Christ of Latter-day Saints, but always essentially a people, just as the communal Jew is more a member of a people than a "church-like" institution. In recent times, however, Mormon leadership has shown impulses to regularize everything, to draw sharp boundaries, to criticize critics, to isolate and ostracize and even excommunicate those who raise questions. In other words, Mormon leadership shows signs of wanting to act like a church.

On the other hand, as Professor Greeley elaborated his theories about "communal" Catholics, a converse idea about Catholicism came to his mind and mine. He has data—Greeley has nothing if he has not data, plus imagination—to show that American Catholicism holds firm as the religion of heritage and choice among one out of every four United States citizens. The number of those who identify their preference as Catholic grows somewhat every year. Greeley can also show that they *like* being thus identified. They enjoy at least selective features of their self-description as Catholics. Yet they are less and less sure about churchly authority, boundaries, and strictures. They are becoming more like what Mormons were and Jews are. So, in formula: while the Mormons were a people and are becoming a church, so Catholicism was (and is) a church but it is also, in significant ways, becoming a people.

This book tries to trace the church and the people through five centuries. It will close with some pointings to trends by an author who knows that historians are not likely to project or guess with much success about the future. He will get more confidence if he feels that readers will pursue further reading, a topic to be introduced by reference to titles I rejected along the way. Here were some plausible possibilities: *American Catholics, American Catholicism, Catholic America, Catholicism in America,* and *American and Catholic*. See how they have been used by others who were in pursuit of descriptness in the American Catholic story.

American Catholics, by James Hennesey (Oxford, 1981) is, with Jay Dolan's new book (see below), one of the two most highly regarded of the comprehensive histories. Hennesey will give readers who wish to pursue the subject significant detail that, were it present here, would distract from the immediate purpose. I avoided reading the general histories while writing this book, for fear of letting my plot be overinfluenced by them or dependent on them. Yet through the years I have been informed by such scholars, and their influence might show even though their pages were not in front of me.

American Catholicism, John Tracy Ellis's miniature classic (University of Chicago, 1969), is two books in one. In its earlier 1955 incarnation, the work evidenced some of the defensive spirit that still came naturally to even this most noted Catholic scholar in what was then "Protestant America." The 1969 update reflects a post-Vatican II ease about the culture and an accompanying concern for the future of the Church after the Second Vatican Council.

Catholic America by John Cogley (Dial, 1973) was a national bicentennial reflection by a noted journalist.

Catholicism in America is a useful anthology edited by Philip Gleason (Harper & Row, 1970).

Robert Leckie's *American and Catholic* is a "good read," a military historian's run-through of the centuries, but is no match for works by professionals like Dolan and Hennesey.

The reference to all these parallels should make clear that my book is about Catholics plus America.

Second, as already mentioned, this is also a story, a history. So its title could have been *The Story of American Catholicism.* Theodore Maynard, however, had used that (Macmillan, 1941) in a pioneering book that is today read only as a period piece. It reveals the older Catholic mentality.

As indicated earlier, while the present book deals only momentarily with Latin and Canadian Catholicism, it focuses largely on the United States. The title could reflect that emphasis. Yet *History of the Catholic Church in the United States* was preempted a hundred years ago by the pathfinder in this field. John Gilmary Shea wrote four still memorable volumes with that title. Or it could have been *The Catholic Church in the United States* by Theodore Roemer (St. Louis, 1950). This book finds few readers today. Much more valuable is Thomas T. McAvoy's, *A History of the Catholic Church in the United States* (Notre Dame, 1969). It is rich in detail but in many respects has been eclipsed by Hennesey and Dolan.

Add "story" or "history," then, to the concept of the book. One could locate other already taken variations, such as *The Catholic Experience: An Interpretation of the History of American Catholicism*. Andrew Greeley already used that one (Doubleday, 1969). It remains well worth reading. A somewhat similar title marks the newest and one of the two best of the comprehensive histories, Jay Dolan's *The American Catholic Experience: A History from Colonial Times to the Present* (Doubleday, 1985). It has the distinction of having the longest title and the opportunity of having profited most from the great increase in research concerning the American Catholic past, research that Professor Dolan has helped stimulate at Notre Dame. Dolan's book has an enviable sweep, and should be just about the first thing anyone should turn to after having read this book.

In those few paragraphs, I have sneaked in a bibliography, a list for further reading, a tool for access to larger data banks. All the mentioned authors, like I, depended upon the detailed monographs and source readings that were made available by other scholars. Dolan, Hennesey, Ellis, and McAvoy cite many of these works, and I direct readers to these larger books as references to the specialized ones.

By now it has to have occurred to a reader: why another "interpretive" "experiential" "story" or "history" of "American" "Catholicism" or of the "Catholic Church" in the "United States" or "America"? A publisher once told me that there must be some visible boon or bounty in a book, something that cannot be gotten elsewhere; otherwise it will not find a readership. What is distinctive?

Here is one obvious and important feature: it is, after five hundred years, the first extended historical essay on American Catholic history by a non-Catholic. Every writer cited thus far was a Catholic. Each was responsible to but by no means necessarily captive of Catholic institutions. Historians are usually hard to take captive. So far, all the general histories of American religion (with the exception of *America: Religions and Religion* by Catherine Albanese) have been written by males from the Protestant culture. No Catholic has yet taken in hand the surveying of non-Catholic American religious history on a grand scale.

Similarly, Protestant historians who included Catholicism in their broad histories were never motivated to write book-length reflections on Catholic history. As a consequence, the field was clear: this is the first book of its sort, from this vantage.

I do not see how such a project could be permanently avoided. Catholics were in America earlier than other Europeans. It is hard to overlook the over fifty million American representatives of the largest Christian group. They are webbed into most chapters of the general histories, like my own recent long story, *Pilgrims in Their Own Land: 500 Years of Religion in America* (Little, Brown, 1984). Yet Catholics look different when they are lifted out for isolated appraisal. That is what I here undertake for the first time.

It is of course no longer a novelty to write a "post-Vatican II" history. Many of the works just mentioned have been of this sort. Yet the overwhelming bulk of documents and assessments in America's 500-year history reflect the experience of a Catholicism very different from the one that we see today. In the United States its chief earlier characteristic was that it was usually beleaguered. "Ghetto Catholicism" was a name for the form that developed in the 100 years before Vatican Council II.

Today, American pluralism is rich and realized. Ecumenism is standard in the national ethos. As a citizen and scholar I participate in pluralism. As a Christian I am a beneficiary of ecumenism. The vantages that come from such a combination inform this book.

While Americans are often accused of having little sense of history, it must be said that Catholics especially neglect their rich history on this continent. Their professional historians are often lonely practitioners. They seem irrelevant to some of the Catholic doers and shapers. Their stories are too rich in contradiction for the simplicists. They are too expressive of human limits to satisfy the pious who would lead-encase their Catholicism. Better days are ahead: we appear to be at a moment when Catholics are beginning to retrieve their past for the sake of their future.

Eugene Goodheart has said of traditions such as this one: you may not possess *it*, but it possesses *you*. Much of life, including church and national life, is involuntary, inherited, "in the genes," as it were: we act upon its signals reflexively. We are limited and haunted by ghostly pasts because they are not really past to us. They haunt us because they are so tantalizingly present. Positively, we devise langages and models for the future. The terms and outlines for these come from the past.

Most of all we are learning something that Theodor Adorno in Germany taught us to see. Since most of human history is made up of suffering, to fail to tell the story of the past is to dishonor the sufferers. People have the potential of growing more humane and richer in empathy as they review both the setbacks and the triumphs of women and men who went before.

My interest, then, is not to let this book be a mere curiosity that would inspire Catholics to "see themselves as others see them." Instead, I hope that my insider/outsider vantage will help Catholics find their identity just as it may help non-Catholics locate American Catholicism and deal with it. History aims to approach such things only very modestly. Yet the search through the past can be informing, reflective, even entertaining at times. I hope this story will be.

Should we call this, then, *An Essay on American Cathoic History?* Because it presents broad outlines rather than confusing details, it takes on the form of essay more than of chronicle. Is it *The American Catholic Search for a Usable Past?* That also matches its intention. I was tempted for a while to call it *An Evening of American Catholic History.* That title did not sound so intimidating. Many, however, might choose to read in the daytime, or through seven or more evenings, not one long one. Yet I would like to have the reader picture us drawing up chairs together and talking about a history that concerns us both, concerns us all.

Let me acknowledge the contribution to my development of the already named people: Professor Dolan and Fathers Hennesey and the late professor Ellis lead that list. The late John Cogley was a friend. Philip Gleason through his essays always nudges me to fresh thought. Andrew Greeley always nudges me to all kinds of thought. To such a list I would have to add, among others, the late Father Colman Barry, O.S.B., who first took me under wing and introduced me to Catholic history. Barry, recalling the initials of his Order of Saint Benedict already back in the 1950s tantalized me. Why not write a biography of the controversial "Angel of the West," with my name, the Benedictine Abbot-Bishop and Indian missionary who had been neglected by the Order? Dare I rush in to treat the man? If so, urged Barry, "Think of the interfaith market for a book titled, *Martin Marty, O.S.B.*, by Martin Marty, S.O.B.!"

I have had quite a number of Catholic doctoral students, and they are making their mark and influencing me. Let me take this moment and space at least to record those "of American Catholic tradition" or those who dealt with American Catholic history in dissertations I have been privileged to advise thus far at the University of Chicago: R. Scott Appleby, Eileen Brewer, Dennis Castillo, Robert Choquette, James Connelley, C.S.C., Peter D'Agostino, Jay P. Dolan, Kathryn Dvorak, Thomas Jonas, Peter Kountz, Joseph McShane, S.J., Beth King McKeown, Stephen Shaw, Mark Sorvillo, Winnifred Sullivan, and Michael Warner. These and scores of other Catholic postgraduates with whom I have worked have, through their researches and our conversations and seminars, left their impact on my thought and immeasurably enriched my life. Mere mention of their names does not do justice to them, but I hope that we have found and will keep finding ways to express our scholarly and personal mutuality.

In 1981, the members of the American Catholic Historical Association honored me by electing me its second (after Albert Outler) non-Catholic president. At that time I learned to know personally dozens of scholars whose works have helped reshape me in mid-career and, hence, helped form the ideas for this book.

My wife, Harriet Marty, has helped in editing this book, after Judy Lawrence had capably processed the words as they came from my word processor. My literary partner, Micah Marty, provided editorial help for this fresh edition. I thank my Divinity School deans, Franklin I. Gamwell and, more recently, W. Clark Gilpin, for the encouragement they have given to this and my other recent scholarly work. My Divinity School, History Department, and History of Culture colleagues also were supportive and keep teaching me. My research assistant Stephen Graham was of great help in the late stages of editing. Finally, the trio of Joel Wells, Todd Brennan, and the late Dan Herr, persisted in urging me to write this and John Sprague nurtured it into this present form. They know that I know that they know the extent of my intellectual, personal, and spiritual debt to them.

Martin E. Marty
The University of Chicago

CHAPTER ONE

Beginnings: 1492-1607

Discovery   The term discovery is controversial, contested, grating to many ears, when applied to what happened when European Catholics ventured to the shores of what became the Americas. Instead, "encounter" came to be the preferred term five centuries after the happenings of 1492. "Discovery" can be seen as insulting. It creates the impression that the people in the Americas had no reason for being, except as those who wait for someone to find them and name them. Because that impression haunts the uses of the term in this context, there are reasons to prefer the idea of "encounters" of two sets of people. Yet, so long as we remain aware of the hazards, we can put the term "discovery," as in "mutual discovery" to good purpose.

One can know or suspect that there were other scriptural writings or carvings for other religions in other cultures before there came to be a book called Genesis in Hebrew Scriptures and thus in the Christian Bible as well. So Genesis is not Genesis

13

to all eyes from all angles, yet it remains as the opening plot line, the setting of the stage for scenes to follow, part of a code to be cracked, an originating word that colors what follows. So as Native Americans encountered Iberian Catholic Christians, and vice versa, they were busy discovering each other, in a pattern that the peoples who were here from before 1492 and those who came from Africa, Asia, and Europe, have been doing ever since. So we can begin with "Discovery" as a kind of "Genesis."

Some may wonder why we begin so far back with a story that does deal much with the space of only those colonies that became what is now the United States for many years. Yet so much of what happened in those first encounters, from 1492 to 1634, colored the subsequent Catholic doings. If some of the story deals with Mexico, Central America, and the Caribbean Islands, we are learning to revisit it while millions of Hispanics, be they Cubans or Puerto Ricans, Mexicans or Central Americans in general, become a part of contemporary American life in general and Catholic life in particular. This old, almost primeval story is intrinsically interesting, but it also helps explain aspects of the Catholic story that were overlooked by non-Latino, non-Latina Catholics and everybody else who told broadly plotted stories.

What we have long called the discovery of America is the one event that all American school children know, or are expected to know. They date the discovery of the New World in 1492. A fine popular instinct protects this date and the name connected with it, Christopher Columbus. Ethnic pride, a passion for historical accuracy, old stone monuments, and other antique traces continually lead to claims for other discoverers. They contend that the Vikings, Bristol fishermen, or Polish pioneers first touched upon the western shores of the Atlantic Ocean.

These adventurers have their place, but they have not won it in the continental myth, with its religious base.

This myth needs Columbus, a man concerning whose achievement folk wisdom and scholarly inquiry agree. Before him, people who were seeking fish or pushing conquest further may well have probed Newfoundland and other shores. The point in all their cases, however, was that no consistent follow up occurred. The written traces are far too meager to permit anyone to do much more than fantasize about what occurred. In the case of Columbus, however, while mysteries and controversies abound, there are also very explicit statements of what was going on in his schemes.

What was going on has gone down in the record books and in popular recall as simply, discovery. Columbus "discovered" America. By his voyages in search of Asia and without knowing it, the Genoan disclosed the existence of a New World. This was half a globe that had been known only to a few million people that we call Native Americans; he, in a monumental act of miscasting, thinking he was in India, called them Indians. The "only" in that sentence sounds condescending. They were not an insignificant set of people who did not matter much then or whose descendants matter even less now. Instead the word reflects the eye and mind of literate peoples who did all the recordkeeping. Chiefly European people framed the outlines of the New World's historic mythology.

Discovery is a term that touches on limitless elements in the human story. Historian and Librarian of Congress Daniel Boorstin even found it plausible to write the history of the whole world around the notion of discovery. His readers and those of many other historians have little difficulty grasping that notion. It suggests horizons, zones which are at the same time signs of the known and the unknown. Queen Isabella of Castile could see a western horizon when first she glimpsed the Atlantic. She at the same time could not "see" all of that horizon, for beyond its limit there seemed to be no limit. A person must find out what is there, both in order to exploit it and to learn what is new in the as yet unseen. Columbus cajoled Isabella for years to let him go seeking, perhaps to discover something. She eventually urged her Aragonese husband Ferdinand—the pope had named the couple the "Catholic sovereigns"—to let Columbus head west to Asia.

The two were grudgingly doing what people in laboratories do when they mix the right chemical elements at the right temperature, then make some mistakes, but thereupon stumble upon something interesting anyhow. The sovereigns' efforts matched those of treasure-seekers. antique shop entrepreneurs, or historians, when any of them rummage through piles seeking one thing and finding something greater. Luck plays its part, though the articulate lay Catholic, Christopher Columbus, would have assigned it all to planning and Providence. The point of it all is not that a certain person turns out to be lucky enough to do the stumbling but that along with serendipity comes new knowledge and newer opportunities. What Columbus himself could not do, a few hundred millions of contemporary and later people have done. They have learned more and made more of what he first discovered and then disclosed without fully knowing what he was doing.

The story of discovery itself is familiar but its outlines need revisiting as regularly as does the Book of Genesis in that grander biblical saga which Columbus thought he was extending. In the beginning, people of vision and enterprise pondered maps. Then they raised money and sailed the seas, sometimes to return with displays of wealth and stories of horror and glory. Among all these, in the fullness of time, there was this Genoa-born adventurer, Cristobal Colon, renamed Christopher, the "Christ-bearer." A truly important and a truly self-important man, he would not be denied. Columbus could both beguile and wear out the patience of monarchs. He could plead abjectly for their support, then walk away, if they denied him, in frustration and disgust; and finally he would return to push for more, if hope for support could be reborn. The Iberian peninsula projects from the European land mass into the Atlantic. Its rulers in the late fifteenth century were shaping their own nations and authorizing Atlantic adventures. Let it be Portugal that got the credit, thought Columbus, if it would put up the money. If not Portugal, let it be—yes, why should it not be?—the Castile and Aragon of the two Catholic monarchs who should live out the purposes of God and Columbus. These purposes easily merged in Colon's Christ-bearing, gold-seeking mind. He insisted that he must be named "Admiral of the Ocean Seas," if successful, as he knew he would be, however much Ferdinand resisted the venture and resented the title. And so it came to be.

In the spring of 1492 the sovereigns and Columbus signed "Capitulations." These made possible his voyages of discovery. With three ships that Isabella found ways to spare, his crews set forth in August. Columbus, very Catholic, always acted in the names of the two figures he invoked on his documents: Jesus and Mary. Yet he took no priests or religious with him. His discovery was a Catholic venture, and a lay one. Columbus was a theologian of sorts, a leader of prayers, a chaplain to his crews. He was capable on shipboard of engaging in the spiritual observances that did not require ordained clergy to be present. That in itself was a mark of his intelligence and devotion. The records of the 1490s suggest that most Europeans had difficulties with both the literary and the spiritual disciplines. The typical lay person could not have interpreted these voyages the way

17

Columbus did, nor expressed the intentions or blessed the ventures with anything like the clarity, the finesse, or the doggedness that he displayed.

What lies beyond horizons, but is open to discoverers, may be vague and endless to some, but his immediate end was simply land. Asian land, let it be, but any land would do. "Land! Land!" Roderigo de Triana's outcry at two in the morning on October 12 signaled that end, and all the subsequent new beginnings. Of course, the Columbian banner that marked the discovery was that of Castile. Also, of course, on it was the cross of Castile, of the Christ-bearer, of Christ. After he returned to Spain, Columbus would twice more probe the American shores that he never knew as anything but Asia. He was an incompetent administrator. Thus he further demonstrated that he was a discoverer. Details of carrying out policy do not always suit the temperaments of adventurers who go on looking for the as-yet-undisclosed. Columbus came back, in the end, in chains. He—the Admiral of the Ocean Seas—died, not truly in glory, in 1506. Besides finding a New World, however, he had by then made his greatest contribution to the myth off which renewers of the world so often live. He was the classic discoverer, who modeled the combination of luck and intention of a sort that, "under God," can move lesser people in his wake and trail.

Crusading

No other word addresses as well the religious side of Columbus's venture. Scholars can spill ink endlessly as they ponder how the religious and the secular elements met in him. They can sort out what aspect represented spiritual striving and what was mere grubbing for gold or reaching for glory. Columbus might not have understood the issue of sorting, since all these impulses and motifs merged in his mind as they did in the minds of so many in his world. People in the late Middle Ages did not always chop things apart and make distinctions the way moderns do, and evidently must. Of course, of *course*, gold and trade were the lures. This goes without saying, but still people say it in order to keep their credentials for sanity. Of course, Columbus would have had no royal backing had he also not been so incautious as to promise grandeur for Spain and wealth for its Catholic sovereigns. What else, however, what equally did he have in mind? The answer, if we take him seriously, is fairly simple. He made it clear enough.

Columbus can well be seen as last in one line of crusaders. Ever after 1095 European Catholics had been taken with a certain fever. They convinced themselves that they must regain the Holy Places in the Holy Land. These were the sacred sites that the infidel boot now profaned and covered over with Islamic signs. With a zeal and madness that defy conventional explanation, sane and otherwise humane men, sometimes women, and, notoriously, once even children, left the discomforts of home and castle for the torture and glory of warfare at the eastern end of the Mediterranean. At first they were seen as pilgrims on a spiritual mission. Then, as the killing went on, until Raymond of Agiles could boast that blood in the streets of Jerusalem flowed to the depth of the horse's ankles, the word "pilgrimage" would no longer do. Now crux, or cross, came to be associated with the campaigns, and "crusades" they became. Crusaders received indulgences from the church. They could die as martyrs and then be transported safely into the realms and range of the vision of God.

By the year 1464 the great crusading phases—most historians count three—were past. In 1453 great Constantinople had fallen and "the Latin states" were lost by Catholics to the Muslim troops. Pope Pius II, who failed in his efforts to regain old lands, or to put boundaries around Ottoman imperial and, hence, Islamic expansion, died in 1464. The Muslim's horse and boot seemed free to trample, and Europe as a whole could not rally against these. One will not easily understand the mentality of adventurers and explorers, or that of the people to whom they appealed, without having some awareness of the psychology of Catholic resentment, of marrow-deep resentment, that came to be mingled with fanaticism and genuine piety.

Some of all this lived in Isabella. Columbus could appeal to it. Intelligent people of the day, like these two, knew that the world was round. They knew that a route to Asia, to "Cathay" and the Indies, would inspire trade. It could also be a combined seaway and highway to the infidel's back door, and to the infidel's therefore stab-worthy back. In his own ways Columbus could promise and, indeed, was promising some that in his graceful whispered pleas and his graceless threats. His western voyages would extend Castile and thus Catholic Spain and expand Christendom. They would thus diminish the realms of the devil and of the enemies of Jesus and Mary. He would not be denied because this vision could not be denied.

Columbus and Isabella, in short, were mystics of a sort and as such were also agents and products of the new reform spirit that issued in this period from what was becoming Spain. St. Teresa of Avila and her kind are better known exemplars of this mysticism: it pushes boundaries, merges human and divine intention and ecstasy, and verges, some think, on heresy. It demands or licenses the notion that leads one to read the human subject confidently into the divine plot and plan. Thus Columbus read himself and the Spain that he flattered and was ready to adopt, for a price. His own notes, a "Book of Prophecies," remove all doubt about his crusading role. In them the explorer jotted some lines about whatever he could know or could dream about "isles far off."

Columbus, like most discoverers, studied old texts and let them begin to disclose what he, by living them out, would extend in new contexts. His choices of such tests strike us as arcane today. He especially favored one of the apocryphal books of Esdras, which most Christians ignore as it lies inert between biblical testaments Old and New. This text made Catholic authority suspicious, because it was so useful to anyone who claimed the prophetic mantle, a garb that worried those who wore mitres or scholars' cloaks. Columbus used this book to show that the world contained more land than water, and that much of this land was yet unknown. On its basis he also made distinctions between various kinds of Jews.

Some latter-day scholars have claimed, thanks to such readings, that he was himself a Jewish-born "New Christian," a disguised convert. Further, the texts helped him speculate about the famed and mysterious Lost Tribes of Israel. Might he help find them after all these centuries? In these texts he also foresaw the prospect of new slaves. (He would later bring some natives back from America, for baptism and slavery. Isabella would have nothing of that. These were her subjects, and Castilian subjects could be no one's slaves!) At this point speculation about Columbus's speculation enters. He left behind some clues that sounded like more than crusading. They better matched the claims of messianism. Was he in his person Esdras's prophesied "man from the sea," "he whom God the Highest hath kept a great season, which by his own self shall deliver his creature" (2 Esdras 13:26)? This is not the place to try to settle the unsettleable about the interior of Columbus's mind. It is the place to address the addressable about the exterior aspects of Columbus's action and to recall the many clues he left. The discoverer related his self-importance to the plans of God for Catholicism and Castile, without ever actually changing those familiar inscriptions, to put "Christ-bearer" next to Mary, where Christ himself already was. The mystic, in the end, can remain orthodox; the messianist can stop short of being Messiah, yet can still be self-driven beyond ordinary claims and boundaries.

The later America that derived from the thirteen colonies on the North American coast was promoted by those who in many cases were sure that they were agents of God. Their acts are inexplicable apart from their notion of a divine "covenant" that made them its agents. They shaped the Protestant, and hence dominant, America for centuries. They also left a conceptual puzzle for Catholics, who find the term "covenant" not so much uncongenial as unfamiliar. The Catholic roots, instead, go back to the idea of crusading. The Protestant notion of the biblical covenant inspired cocksureness. It ruled out too many people, beginning with the heathen Indian, and eventually degenerated into mere Yankeehood. Yet it also helped produce a popular sense of worth. From it came frequent calls for people to invest in a history that God endowed with meaning.

Similarly, the Catholic notion of the crusade is not necessarily lovely, whether in international affairs or when exercised in support of orthodox teaching or enforced practical action. It certainly worked against the "pagan" Native American as much as the covenant ever did. One would find it hard to build a republic or a world of Christian ecumenical, interfaith, or international scope on the basis of crusading. Whoever reaches back for Catholic roots, however, will necessarily come back to see in American origins something of the crusading vision of Columbus and his sponsoring Queen. They successfully helped endow the westward ventures with spiritual purpose and religious interpretations, for better and for worse. Naturally, the discoverer named his landing place "San Salvador," Holy Savior, and *not* "El Dorado," the place of Gold. He was on a holy mission.

Encounter   No other word better describes what the discoverers left behind in Spain and faced ahead in America. No word better indicates the biggest difference between the way the American Catholic story was once told and the way it now must be. Once that story was conventionally seen as having begun in 1634 in Maryland. There the account of Catholicism in the thirteen English colonies had its original start. The story of Portuguese, Spanish, and French beginnings between 1492 and English settlement in 1607 belonged, then and there, to prehistory. The achievements of Hispanic Catholicism and Hispanic America do not permit such a late-rooted account that would overlook or deny the beginnings. Tourists who have visited California, all the Southwest, and Florida, can make little sense of the missions and forts and ruins if these all represent a mere prelude to the real history. Too many survivals of the early Mediterranean-era Catholicism are visible. They permit no such ignoring or intentional obscuring of roots. There are also continuities, especially in the primal narratives and myths, that connect those times and ours.

Such insights were long obscured because of a prevailing, still contending countermyth. This one suggests that a person can tell the Catholic story apart from its environmental contexts. The church was not lead-encased, hermetically sealed from other forces in history. Its story was not just one of a hierarchy and a set of priests and religious. Nor could it continue as simply an account of a missionary church that existed in a European vacuum, mysteriously transported across the Atlantic to a virgin, empty land.

No, the Old World was itself rich in context and competition, full of religions. The New World, while sparsely settled, was also "full" of peoples who converged precisely at these same choice sites—the mouths of rivers, the defensible hills—that Europeans chose for their own.

Therefore on both shores were stories, not of protected Catholics, but of Catholics in encounter. The encounters were, as often as not, military and strategic. They were, almost as often as not, puzzling. They led to bemusement and stupefaction on all sides. It was hard in that century for people to consider their interactions as "interfaith dialogues." It still is, except in a few sheltered nations and on privileged occasions. Someone who is today conceived to be a dialogue partner then was often a thing, an object called an infidel, heathen, and pagan—or, a bit later, when northern and Protestant Europe came on the scene as a rival, a heretic. Whatever forms these took, and a few were partly civil, they were vivid encounters. Scholars have to take into account the eyes and intentions of the "other," the partners and antagonists in such engagements.

On the European, African, and Middle Eastern side, all this had meant that Christians must encounter Islam and Judaism. Thus it had been chronically for centuries, and so it had become acute. The year 1492 was a turning point but not an interruption in the larger history. How anyone in the past could try to get away with telling the story apart from Catholic entanglements with Islam may seem itself to be as great a mystery as are many of the details of that story itself. Certainly the Muslim was on the mind of Catholic Europe's plotters and planners. One might notice, for example, that a bit later, around 1517, the northern European Protestant reformers got away with many of the rebellious activities because the pope and his allies were preoccupied. They were busy and on guard against that "Turk" or Muslim who would advance from the East on Vienna, and almost did so successfully.

That was the eastern half of an imperial pincers, whose western half concerns the present story. Even after Islam took rise in the seventh century under Muhammad, the prophet of Allah, this passionate spiritual rival to Catholicism threatened from Africa and within a century had taken part of what today is Spain. From there the Muslim always threatened to capture more of Europe. For some centuries various kinds of coexistence developed in Spain, and Jews were thrown in to this tense and creative mix for good measure. Religions then as they often do now lived with the notion that they needed space: Christendom abutted what is now dubbed Islamdom. Both tried to sequester the Jews, who were allowed no "-dom," no domain. The Christians eventually tried to put Jews out.

As for the Muslims on Iberian soil, they were to be subjects of a *Reconquista*, of Catholic efforts to reconquer those lands they had lost in the eighth century. When, beginning in the eleventh century, these Muslims, or Moors, stopped presenting a united front, Christians made their counter moves. The Moors were in no position casually to fold their tents and obligingly to move on. Indeed, they had erected grand mosques and other edifices which still stun visitors. They inspire awe because of their beauty and their implications of potency. The basic encounters between the peoples came to be military. After almost two centuries *Reconquista* meant that Islam was being sequestered in a few enclaves in and near Granada.

The encounters never led to spiritual appreciation between these two monotheistic faiths. There were some major intellectual exchanges. Many elements in later Catholic thought arrived there thanks to philosophical gifts handed over often unwittingly by Muslim scholars. For the most part, a divided and weakened Islam was vulnerable to a uniting and strengthened Catholic Spain. It is often pointed out that when encounters of conflict are attractive or necessary, it becomes expedient to hate the enemy and to love the ally. It had always been easy to hate the Muslim because of the aggressiveness in the Islamic claims and policies. Also, this was true because the Muslim story in the Holy Qur'an paralleled and then undercut the distinctive biblical stories of Abraham, Moses, Mary, and Jesus, by seeing them not as final norms but in a mere sequence that climaxed in the last prophet, Muhammad.

The expedience of allying and loving the ally was an idea that was a bit harder to promote. Strictly speaking there was as yet no Spain but only a set of rival provinces. Ferdinand and Isabella, by their marriage in 1469, were both the beneficiaries and promoters of a new spirit. It would unite Spain to the glory of God, the Catholic Church, and a rising empire. Granada, meanwhile, looked vulnerable, and was. Ferdinand and Isabella therefore began the necessary mopping-up operations to finish clearing the peninsula and inventing Spain. They both became familiar figures at battle sites. They knew enough to acknowledge God in their often successful ventures. Isabella was fired by a zeal for God. Hers was a new style of piety that led her to choose the reformist course of Cardinal Cisneroz de Ximenez over corrupt and corrupting compromisers.

The Queen then compromised her own many and obvious virtues by taking part in reestablishing the Inquisition, or establishing the *Spanish* Inquisition. It was the most feared heresy-hunting project in Catholic history, all in the name of piety and unity.

Granada fell early in 1492. Columbus seemed to wait only hours before attempting again to attract the attention of the long-distracted Catholic sovereigns back to his crusading project. Their preserved capitulations and agreements with him read as simply secular and materialistic documents. They spoke only of merchandise and merchandising, of goods and business. The parties to the contracts did not need to say more. A united Spain could henceforth concentrate also on having an empire by plundering Asia and the seas. Yet there lingered another distraction, the symbol of another long encounter.

In 1492 it was the Jew who remained to plague those who desired to see and form a united Catholic Spain. That year is almost as large in Jewish history as it is for Western history in general, but for a tragically different reason. Ferdinand and Isabella that year drove Jews into exile. Some of the last of them to flee may have been visible in the ports as Columbus left for his Atlantic explorations. Ever since earliest Christian times Catholics had turned Jews into victims and enemies, into virtual things instead of letting them be their own persons. Like the Muslims, Jews had different and undercutting versions of the very events and meanings that made up salvation and singular truth for Catholics.

Through the years before and during the *Reconquista* Jewish fortunes varied, often depending upon the attitudes of the predominant other two sets of peoples and their faiths. Spanish soil had become the site of one of the greatest Jewish cultures or civilizations ever known. This civilization had developed through mutual if wary encounters between peoples. Yet as the passion for Catholic orthodoxy and Spanish unity grew, Jews became first luxuries and then mere objects of revulsion. Many of them converted, often because they accepted as true the Christian story held by their neighbors and perhaps just as often because it was expedient to do so. These became "New Christians," or "Marranos," probably because that word connoted pigs, the animal prohibited among Jews.

The Inquisition was aimed not at Jews as Jews but at New Christians who were presumed to be possible heretics. Its methods left the accused defenseless. It initially became a problem and then a terror for the New Christians. They might be betrayed by their rivals or by their own reflexive actions; a mere gesture remembered from Jewish worship and ways could be incriminating. By 1492 the idea of exile seemed almost a relief, though an appalling version of it, to Jews who had lived suspect or died innocently for decades.

New Christians almost certainly played major parts in the story of the American adventure. Luis de Santangel, a Queen's treasurer who arranged for Isabellan funding, is believed to have been one. So were certain hierarchs and, possibly, de Triana, who first spotted American land. Because of things Columbus wrote familiarly about, regarding Esdras and prophecy and Jews, and for other reasons, as we have noted, some people in our time, not all of them reckless—one thinks of the great Spanish writer Salvador de Madariaga, for instance—have proposed the idea that the discoverer Columbus was himself one.

Be all those suggestions what they may, the reality was that Catholic Spain cruelly put out those Jews that it had not hounded or persecuted, all in the name of negative encounter, of national and religious purity and unity. Latter-day Catholics who work for positive relations with Jews have come to learn that the story of Spain, 1492, haunts their Jewish partners and remains vivid in their tradition. From Spain some Jews fled for a time to Portugal only to be betrayed, and thence to Brazil, and thereupon to New Netherland—New York to us—in 1654. Others enriched the lands of the Turk or established themselves in the ghettos of London, Amsterdam, or eastern Europe. There were no happy chapters in Catholic-Jewish relations in this period.

Another encounter remained ahead for Columbus and his successors. This involved those occupants of the American lands that they often considered empty, and thus Spain's. These were people they thought were the Lost Tribes of Israel, or else heathens, pagans, poor souls, if they were souls at all. They had been hidden for millennia by the devil in the previously unknown world that was becoming the New World. We know little from the Native Americans' side of what they thought of the Spanish newcomers, since these people could not write. We have to deduce from their actions what they thought. Sometimes they would briefly accommodate the intruders and invaders. More often they resented the doubling up and piling on of peoples in places that they themselves already cherished. In such cases the natives could be as cruel and revengeful torturers as were their conquerors.

We know chiefly what the new people from Europe thought. Columbus, the man of God and gold, left behind the primal perception. This means that many who followed him acted upon both parts of his understanding. First, the Arawaks on the island he named San Salvador were possessed of souls. It was on that perception that missionaries acted, especially when they agreed with him that the "Indians do not hold any creed nor are they idolaters; but they all believe that power and good are in the heavens. . . ." They seemed to be a people of a "very acute intelligence," and were "guileless and generous with all that they possess. . . ." They did have another, a savage, side, these people of the Indies, but that did not need to show the first day. The Noble Savage was born in this paragraph; only his naming remained to be applied by Europeans who read such accounts of these early encounters.

The other paragraph recalling the earliest days was more ominous. Columbus and the Europeans never doubted their superiority or their rights over these presumed Asians who, it should have been assumed, would have their own concepts of their dignity. For one thing, Columbus announced that while he found no human monstrosities, he did hear that some ate human flesh. Worse, for them, he deduced that these Indians might serve the Christians. This meant they could be slaves. The Christians made ceaseless efforts to make them such.

Those Columbian letters provide tantalizing pristine glimpses of a sort that are rarer than one might wish. All too soon the Caribbean and Central-South American killing and enslaving began, and encounters did not remain free and open. The Native Americans were on the defensive and when they took counter-measures, such Indians roused only negative imagery. Remember: it is expedient to hate the enemies, to recreate them in the form of any convenient stereotype.

The invented native was part Noble Savage, part intelligent guileless/guileful counterpart, sometime monster and cannibal, ofttime idolater and at least heathen and pagan. Given the quick forming of those types in mind and eye, the first thing that had to go was any positive view of their ritual, their myths and symbols, the passages of life, their motives for generosities, their modes of belonging to each other—in short, their religion. The earlier Catholic history followed this suppressive model. It is now being retold, as it must be retold, in the light of some almost forgotten positive encounters. In the academy this recovery means the use of the disciplines of History of Religion or phenomenology of religion. With them comes a sympathetic eye for what natives did and believed. Sometimes it even leads to the point of latter-day white self-hate. This approach allows for no good in the exploitative, imperialistic conquerors who never show up as Catholic believers who were filled with conflicting hopes and fears and ambiguities.

Given the newer curiosities and motivations, storytellers reach for records like those of Columbus in the earliest days. There are a few samples of the sort that delight anthropologists and appreciators of religion. Among these, for instance, is a *relación* of Alvar Nuñez Cabeza de Vaca. He was one of the less fortunate wanderers of the time, whose wandering turned out to be fortunate for anyone who wishes to glimpse Native American life as if at first hand.

Much had happened in the four decades before Cabeza de Vaca came on the scene. Columbus himself never touched United States soil. The first Spaniards to do so were in the party of Ponce de Leon, who landed on Easter Day of 1513, at a flowery place they spoke of as Pascua Florida—it is just Florida, to us. Ponce de Leon was to lose his life in Florida in 1521, thanks to an Indian arrow. He was one among many who wanted to conquer, govern, and missionize that great peninsula. Cabeza de Vaca was treasurer of an expedition in 1536 under the failure-prone conqueror, Panfilo de Narváez. The story of Narváez's mishaps can bring laughter and tears, but on the pages of others, not here. We need only rescue the sight of Cabeza de Vaca and three companions, one of them a Moor, and then watch them proceed. On land and Gulf sea, among Indian "tribe" after tribe, as tricksters and healers, slaves and escapees, men of hope and despair and constant pluck, Cabeza de Vaca and companions were observers who tried to leave an honest (but necessarily left a garbled) account of what and who they saw along the way.

"We passed through many and dissimilar tongues. Our Lord granted us favor with the people who spoke them, for they always understood us, and we them." *Somehow*, one adds tentatively; *maybe*, one must add. The wanderers did become linguists of a sort. This was especially true of the Moor Estevanico, who also, though not himself a Christian, learned how to effect healings by using the sign of Jesus' cross.

Along the way the party observed rituals that both moved them and frightened them. They became aware of curiosities like Indian homosexuality and alert to stories of golden cities. No scholar today can with confidence sort out the clusterings that we call tribes from each other. Yet one impression is clear: in open encounter the natives had something to offer. Cabeza de Vaca believed they could be won by kindness, not by conquest. His way, of course, was not to be extensively tried. His record, however, calls to mind the fact that Native Americans did have their own religions and effective ways of dealing with the environment, each other, and healers or slaves, victims or friends, like Cabeza de Vaca and Estevanico, in their midst. They remain a strong part of the story, not shadows at its edge.

Conquest

By now little more need be said about this most obvious feature of relations between Europeans and Native Americans: conquest. Columbus assumed that he would have the right to add Asian lands to Catholic Spain and the pope's empire. It became even more clear to his successors that by right they could have the gold and the lands if, first, they would conquer. So they have come down into history not as discoverers, explorers, adventurers, missionaries, or investors, though some were each of all these things. Instead they have the group name "Conquistadores."

These were military people, sometimes fools, sometimes valiants on heroic scales. They readily used their Catholic faith to legitimate their plunder and to bring comfort to themselves in their failures. And there were failures. The stories of almost mythical types like the Cortezes as victors are well known. Less remembered are the utter failures like Narváez and Ponce de Leon and, more notably, Hernando de Soto. To de Soto, Indians were simply in the way, to be exploited or killed. They and the environment bested him and his kind.

Taking for granted their rights to what were known now no longer as the Indies but as the New World of the Americas, some early sixteenth-century Spaniards touched on most of the states that border the Gulf, plus today's New Mexico, Arizona and California. Best remembered of these was Coronado, who after 1540 tried to fulfill the dreams of Estevanico and of the strange liar or madman, Fray Marcos de Niza. This man of God was sure he had glimpsed golden cities in the Southwest's sun. Like all others on United States soil, Coronado failed as Conquistador, his party having penetrated all the way into what is today Kansas.

In the company of such venturers, there were, as we shall see, also some more humane friars, brothers, religious, who, without ever granting equal rights or status to natives, showed their own kinds of love in their own kinds of ways. They chose the way of conquering that de Vaca had prescribed. It never had much chance so long as the prospect of gold and governorships was so alluring among Conquistadores. A new interaction did, however, begin to develop between these priests or religious and the Spanish plunderers. They expressed a decisive reaction that spurred them to change. It began with tears.

Weeping

As so often in religious, specifically Jewish-Christian, history, the turnings—repentance, renewal, resolve—began with weeping for the self and for others. Catholics who look for better chapters in their early New World saga find these not when cocksure messiahs read themselves into scriptures or when conquerors sharpened their swords. Instead, those who wept for what the plunder did to Indian victims and Spanish souls now receive higher regard from their legatees.

Weeping and sympathy, for instance, led Juan de Padilla to be the first of 116 Catholic martyrs on North American soil. To the historians of religion, martyr may not seem an appropriate term. What business did this man of the Christian God have on the soil of Quivira? He simply suffered for being a partner to those who saw Quivira as an El Dorado of their dreams. He was a kind of chaplain to the conquerors, wasn't he? He was, and if life came in neat packages de Padilla could be dismissed as a guileless but still guilty co-Conquistador. Yet things were more complex than that. One is reluctant to take away his title because of revised assumptions about human roles.

Juan de Padilla evidently kept looking back over his shoulder in regret as Coronado had to turn back in disgrace. By now the missionary had come to care for, one might even say to love, these Native Americans. He thought that by his ministering he might bring some of those souls to heaven, beyond the reach of foolish conquerors. Padilla eventually found means to make his way back to where he had taught Indians to revere a cross. On his return he was moved and charmed to see that they regarded its base as a sacred site to be swept and kept clean. His misfortune came when the demand for missionaries outpaced supply. Tribes vied for his service, evidently believing his powers to be magical. They feared lest their enemies might profit from his ability to transact with unseen powers. In their rivalry, he was killed and his body dumped into a ravine. Others in his small party were also to be killed or to disappear. One is tempted to make much of coincidence in symbols associated with their death. Draw a cross, with the horizontal bar half way up the map of the forty-eight states and the vertical half way between east and west of these coterminous United States. A few miles from where the lines meet, at the nation's heart, is the spot that marks the first to fall, Padilla, one who wept for the Indians.

Better remembered in this role was a man who like Columbus never touched United States soil. He was a Columbus biographer and a man for the ages, Bartolomeo de Las Casas. The Catholic saga of the Americas includes few of his kind at the beginning. Las Casas, however, makes it into the gallery of heroes though not saints, not because the competition was so slight but because of the grandeur of his merits and the irony of his flaws. He lived long and wrote much. A Las Casas scholarly club of sorts can quote the great historian Samuel Eliot Morison who nominated Las Casas' *Historia de las Indias* to be the most treasured of all the colonial historical writings. Of course, Las Casas was a failure as a protector of the Indians. He was royally assigned and he chose to have the role of weeper, yet, be it insisted, he was anything but weepy. He was a doer, a busy dreamer-up of Utopias for Latin American places. Las Casas attracted enemies of note on both sides of the Atlantic, and their quality is a mark of the man on his own.

A Sevillean born around 1474 and a guardian soldier at Granada five years after it fell, he had come to the West Indies by 1502. Las Casas received a land grant and took holy orders. Some say he was the first Catholic in America to be ordained as a priest. The priest had known of slaveholding conquerors who lined Indians in rows to make shooting more efficient, lest ammunition be wasted. On August 15, 1514, having seen more misery and murder of natives than he could stand, he preached on a text that convinced him he should weep and repent and lead others to do the same. The sermon's text said one should not even live off the labor of others to say nothing of killing them. He must free his serfs; so should others. The timing was good.

The pope was working for better conditions; Archbishop Ximenez was of similar sentiment. A mixture of people in Spain found motives to work for "New Laws" that would moderate New World conditions. Such change would be a threat to people of New World wealth and to the clergy who favored them, so Las Casas came to be on the spot.

He began to commute across the Atlantic, and was given backing for some experimental colonies which, predictably, failed to provide new models for Indian living. In 1523, after Las Casas became a Dominican, he began a career of retreat and attack in the public forum on the basis of his devotion and scholarship. In respect to encounters with native faiths, he was distinctive: he would evangelize peacefully and show regard for Indian ways.

So striking were Las Casas' attacks, so rich their documentation, that the English were later to use them to fashion a "Black Legend" that accused Spain of special cruelty. The legend helped England gain moral credibility for New World ventures but did not lead these men of the North to adopt happier policies toward the Native Americans. Las Casas had his own eye on higher goals: in 1550 at Valladolid in Spain he debated Juan Gines de Sepulveda, an Aristotelian who set out to show that Indians were natural inferiors to whites. Las Casas had the better of the argument but less effect on the consequences. Indian slavery had been too firmly rooted. By the time of his death in 1566 he had come to be recognized as Catholic Europe's most eloquent and discerning defender of rights, seeker of justice, and worker for peace in the newly discovered hemisphere. Any New World Catholic human rights movement, be it in North or South America, legitimately traces roots back to Las Casas.

Fortunately for those who are put off by mere sainthood or Manichaean views of history in which God's good folk are perfect and the devil's bad ones are nothing but imperfect, Las Casas revealed a cosmic flaw of the sort most saints also displayed in their revealing autobiographies. In his case, this meant a very brief moment in which, unfortunately for them, he supported the idea of importing blacks to replace the Indian serfs that he would free in the Americas. Such incongruities are hard to explain except when one sees Las Casas not as a twentieth-century heir of long-term civil rights discussions but as a half-finished product at a moment when slavery was still taken for granted, as it had been immemorially, through the millennia. The priest soon repented of his proposal, but it was fateful and unfortunate, to say the least, for Africans. This is not to say that black slaves were in America because of Las Casas. It is to say that some defenders of Negro slavery salved their consciences or pointed to others' inconsistencies by citing Las Casas.

Why associate this active, argumentative man with a presumably passive, acquiescent response like weeping? The answer is simple: he wept. The pope officially named him protector of the Indians and Las Casas unofficially defined that role as one that began in crying for their suffering and fate. It is often said that the aggressive covenants of Christian life, especially American style, allow for no softness, no vulnerability. Yet Las Casas, in what was still an almost totally male cast, in a world that one day would be described as *macho*, showed the courage and strength to weep for others, for himself.

Las Casas, believed by some in our time to have been a "New Christian," took risks by defending Jews and urging that they and Muslims had rights to live on Catholic soil. This was a dangerous doctrine, given the times. He further helped establish the image of "Christ-bearer" Columbus in a biography that re-imaged his hero. Parishioners in what is today Guatemala all but lynched him when he as their bishop at Chiapas tried to discipline slaveholders. He made a fool of himself in some of his communitarian experiments. He was inconsistent and had not considered the consequence of some of the causes he was called on to promote. A person who stood between the times, as it were, one who stood on moral horizons, he set a precedent that was often neglected by later prophets and activists. First, and most of all, he always identified with the victims. He wept.

Mission

Hovering over or implied in all these accounts of the humane religious men who accompanied the Conquistadores is the word "mission." Five centuries later it has become difficult first for anthropologists and History of Religion students, with their creditable interest in religious parity and underdog peoples, and then for all but the most assertively witnessing Catholics, to get inside the minds of those who set out to convert. So they were the chaplains to empire builders and plunderers. Should they not have stayed home in Europe? Would it not have been more moral for Catholics to work for change on the Spanish or, later, French side of the water rather than to bestir Franciscans and Dominicans and, later, Jesuits to come to the New World and imply that their ventures could be moral?

Once voiced, such questions pile up. Those who find easy answers perhaps have not thought much about the subject. Who, for instance, gave the right to try to convert anyone at all to even the de Vacases and Las Casases, the men who advocated voluntary conversions alone? There was enough nobility in the Noble Savages, enough Indian respect for spirits and Spirit, for ancestors and tribe and nature, to permit others to affirm their value systems—at least as much as one might affirm those of Cortez or Sepulveda. What permitted Europeans to interrupt other cultures that they must have known and shown to be militarily inferior? Did they measure the pain of Indian families in upheaval when some members went the Catholic way while others stayed with the old rites? The reality of being converted often went along with moving to one of the Catholic missions of the sort whose remains or reconstructions one can still see all along the California trail. Such relocating benefited those who were protected by mission walls and ways, but it was disruptive of the ordinary economy. Maybe it was true that priests and friars embarrassed some military leaders. They slowed down owners of silver mines in the Southwest by protesting their slave economy. Yet even for them to be on the scene intending to change, civilize, or educate these Native Americans is an ideal that runs counter to assumptions about what mission should be today.

Rather than extend the list indefinitely or to apologize for the missionaries, the historian writing an essay has a different task. It begins with the proposition that the story will not be told or understood outside the context of possibilities that were available to people in the past. Catholics of the sixteenth century had known little of the Renaissance, nothing of the Enlightenment or Interfaith Relations or History of Religions and anthropological scholarship. They would not even have comprehended a civil argument which contends that they provided some alternative order and humane living while the conquerors were destroying all the old order in inhumane ways.

The evangelizers and missionaries held a simple ideology and faith. It led them sometimes to yearn for martyrdom and to gain it. They acquired bedsores and saddlesores and footsores on their road in efforts to win Indians. They took risks, and had to park some of their intelligence at the mission's door as they traded trinkets and invented devices that would make the Christian story vivid to Native Americans. Such men of great intelligence like Las Casas and, along the way, Eusebio Kino and Junipero Serra are not explainable on ordinary scales. They were beneficiaries of the best that Europe had to offer by way of science and humane learning. While students, they would orient or occident their living quarters, as Kino did in Austria at seminary, in order to help them concentrate on the Asians and Indians that they would win. So what did motivate them?

The only sustainable answer for such varied thousands of people in sundry religious orders was this: the reality of heaven and hell, a life of rewards and punishments after this one, was as real to them as was the temporal world to those around them. They believed the New Testament commands that promised salvation and heaven to the baptized believers and threatened hell to those who were unbaptized and did not believe. Only Las Casas once went so far as to say that a person did an infant no favor saving him from hell yet letting him drown during baptism. Yet Las Casas saw these to be false alternatives. If pushed to choose, he would have chosen heaven rather than extended earthly life for the child.

Catholics were better missionaries than the Protestants who arrived later. Theirs was a faith based not so much on literacy and critical judgment about texts as was Protestanism. Their faith was full of tangible, visible, dramatic reminders and rituals. They could connect Catholic beads and bells and crosses, its wine and water and signs of the cross, with a world open to Indian imagination long before the natives learned to read. When Juan de Padilla and 115 others met their deaths, or when Cabeza de Vaca kept shedding skin under the parching Rio Grande Valley sun; when Las Casas risked his neck before the lynch mob and thousands of priests braved unutterably remote and depressing loneliness, they knew exactly why they were doing what they were doing. And when Indian raiders burned the missions, and when *Reconquista*-minded natives like a man named El Popé led rebellions that forced the retreat by whites, the missionaries abandoned their missions in tears. Yet names were being written in the book of life. It may not be possible or valid to try mentally to reenact such understandings in intercultural contacts today, or wherever evangelizing goes on. It is all but impossible to understand the actions of brother this and father that apart from seeing them finding themselves in a fateful cosmic drama. This drama put them, far from civilization, at the center of motion and meaning in history.

Settlement   When Spaniards began to put down stakes and roots, a new chapter begins. The great History of Religion expert Mircea Eliade has written that the act of settling in a place consecrates it. So long as one sets out only to discover, explore, conquer, or plunder, his relation to an environment is profane. One who uses a place, but is not of it, does not dedicate it. Many of the transactions between Conquistadores and Native Americans, between silverminers and the old landholders in Europe, were spiritless, a mere taking of advantage. Eventually some Spaniards said that the way to understand the New World, to be fair to it and to themselves economically, to save and serve the Indians, was to begin permanent homes. Then, first, was the kind of consecration of which Eliade speaks. Catholic America can look well behind and beyond the conventional actors on the American colony stage, the Pilgrims and Puritans of 1620 and 1630 or, before them, the Jamestown Virginians of 1607, to the initial permanent settlements. These were Catholics.

There had to be failures, first. In 1570 a Spanish vessel sailed into Chesapeake Bay, then more ardently named the Bay of the

Mother of God, to the same James River that later hosted Jamestown Anglicans. A party of five Jesuits, three brothers and two priests, plus some novices, a stray boy, and an Indian guide, landed there. It was they, under Juan Baptista de Segura, who wanted to convert the land we now call Virginia.

The Indian guide, a captive of Spaniards who had been educated in Spain, was to assist the venture. He too much enjoyed reversion to the ways he had earlier left under force. In a plot that was often to be reenacted and, hence, was predictable, he moved back to his own people. It was found that he had over-advertised the crop potential of the area, and thus had inconvenienced the Jesuit pioneers. Yet the Catholics set about their work. When word came that this Indian had lapsed, as the Jesuits would put it, the missionaries set out to retrieve him for Catholic faith and European ways. Their guide, when approached, was courteous enough to return with them, but it turned out that he had arranged a ruse. The party was ambushed. One priest and two brothers were killed. A few days later the guide and his colleagues engaged in a second ruse. This time they were given axes, and used them on the rest of the Catholics. The colonial effort thus ended. Only the Spanish boy was spared, but taken captive. A year later a party from Florida came to take revenge, and executed some Indians, but they left Virginia as it had been and would be for a third of a century more: beyond the scope of Christendom.

Honors for place as the oldest settlement went instead to Florida, as any visitor to rebuilt Saint Augustine would know. In 1565 the capable Pedro Menendez de Aviles, an admiral, was sent by King Philip II to start a colony where so many had already failed, in Florida. Far from being a mere conqueror, he came equipped with a large party of Franciscans and Jesuits who were to fan out through Florida for missions. They began to do so. On September 8, St. Augustine's day, Menendez affixed the saint's name to his chosen fortress site. Here at last there was to be some success.

Holy War   Let it also be said that from St. Augustine one caught a momentary glimpse of Holy War, on the European model. This was a conflict pattern that, happily for later America, never took hold. For ages, when two species of religion crowded a space, they treated each other the way biological species do if they favor the same food. One must get rid of the other.

By the 1560s some European reformers who did not follow the Catholic patterns typified by Ximenez and Isabella, by the Inquisition or the Jesuits, an order founded by Ignatius Loyola, had enjoyed two generations of progress. Heirs of Martin Luther in Germany, Huldreich Zwingli in Switzerland, and Frenchman John Calvin in Switzerland and France and the Lowlands, they had broken with Rome and already had begun conflict with each other. Their reform centered in an attack on the hierarchical system. They believed this to be an enslaving pattern by which the church held people to fear of hell and the earning of heaven. The people who were called Protestant insisted that they alone offered the free grace in Jesus Christ. Instead of the pope they would follow the authority of the Bible and conscience. In France the party of Protestants, often miscalled "Lutherans" by Spaniards, were Calvinists, or Huguenots. Often they were highly placed people, members of French elites.

Some Huguenots, under René de Laudonnière and Jean Ribaut, foreseeing the need for a place for exile and seeing the need for land investment, in 1564 had founded a colony at the St. John's River mouth north of St. Augustine. The colonists' company was not purely Protestant. It was anything but purely religious in scope as its leaders set up housekeeping within its barricades. The colony was properly perceived as a threat to Catholic Florida. If Florida was strategic to Menendez de Aviles, who was assigned the task of protecting Spanish gold shippers, the place could also become so to France, to Huguenots, to anyone who might wish to subsidize a colony or a government for a year by pirating a galleon or two. The faith of the Huguenots provided the greater emotional if not strategic threat to Catholics. Menendez de Aviles, a strong and wily man, engineered a plot from St. Augustine. Within days he attacked by land and sea. Breaking the codes of honor of a later day but living by those of his own, he offered the prospect of life to captives—and then had their heads. At St. Augustine on September 6 the priests held a Mass and led the singing of the *Te Deum* to recognize the act of killing "Lutherans." Several years later, France, not only Huguenot France, replied in kind and attacked St. Augustine, with a goal of evening the numbers of heads taken. So it had been in Europe. So would it be in America.

For a complex of reasons, however, while war between European powers would extend to the New World, and while anti-Protestant or anti-Catholic sentiment might fuse and fire "secular" wars that would have occurred anyhow, Holy War did not become a precedent or pattern. Could it be that the lesson about the futility of Holy War was too recently learned to make such war attractive? Were secular motives themselves sufficient, apart from religion, to license killing? Could it be that the American landscape was simply so vast that busy settlers could be far enough apart not to bother, not to have to bother, each other? Were new ideas of tolerance being born?

The unfolding story of colonizing provides some answers to such questions. Here it is important to note only that the first would-be permanent French and the first permanent Spanish settlements (where the United States would be) went to war, and that ended that. Late in the twentieth century a person reads of more violence *per day* in the Iranian jihads, in Hindu, Muslim, and Sikh conflict, or in Muslim-Jewish based warfare in the Middle East than has occurred in *more than four centuries* on colonial and then United States soil. Violence, often verbal, there would be. Usually it was ulcer-inducing or undignified conflict, but Holy War? Seldom.

Folk Faith   It is not necessary to trace in detail the other story of settlement, but it demands mention in order to draw attention to the main theater of Catholic engagement, in the Southwest. St. Augustine aside, all other sites for pilgrims who followed the Catholic trail lie between Texas and California. The pioneer here was Don Juan de Onate, a Creole who began colonizing after having made his mint in Mexican mines. He included ten missionaries in his military company of 400, a company that included 7,000 head of cattle. To second the St. Augustine motion, he founded San Juan, near a village of Tewa Indians. He pressed on from there to Kansas and California, engaging in conflict with Indians but getting little reward for his efforts. The Mexican Viceroy lost interest in New Mexican investments and the troubles they evoked among Apache, Comanche, and other warlike tribes. Onate gave up, was all but fired, and it was left to Pedro de Peralta to found a new capital, a place that endures as Santa Fe. Its Governor's Palace is the oldest public building in America.

Santa Fe did not boom. It was more a military base than an investment hub or marketing center. The city remains more important for what it contributed to missions, since a generation of evangelizers spread out from there. By 1625, before the time that the Massachusetts Bay Puritans began to arrive, there were 43 missions around Santa Fe in New Mexico. Indian souls counted for much. Mass baptisms occurred. The bookkeepers counted over 30,000 Christian Indians. They may not have understood the faith in the way literate Europeans might have preferred, but much of Europe's was also a folk faith. Some historians see it as its own kind of paganism overladen with Christian symbols. Articulate and clarified versions of the faith belonged chiefly to elites: friars, professors, some priests, and nobles among the laity. On such terms, the Indian response may not suffer as much by comparison. The Catholic ritual and the routines of mission life held their lures.

Ritual   One cannot commendably close the book or chapter on the earliest Catholic beginnings without noticing how much public ritual characterized life among discoverers, in settlements and colonies. This search could take the form of Columbus stopping for Mass as he left Spain, or listening to the chants in the monasteries as he put out to sea. Or it could be known in the services of prayer he led on shipboard. When a new "governor" would come to a place like Florida, he would convoke an assembly of uncomprehending natives and read to them, or into the air, royal sounding authorizations from monarch or pope. A *Te Deum* must follow the victory of Menéndez de Aviles upon his return to St. Augustine.

Juan de Padilla had observed the ritual sweeping at the foot of the cross in Quivira. Cabeza de Vaca's party made the sign of the cross during their long wandering. Almost at once, in Santo

Domingo and Haiti and Mexico and elsewhere, cathedrals rose to house the Mass. Baptisms were the main means of access by missionaries to the mentalities of Native Americans. Naming was also important. Pascual Florida was an ideal designation for the first place touched, on an Easter day. San Salvador suggested the power of names and naming, as did all the St. Augustines and San Juans dedicated to saints. Santa Fe means "holy faith," and was a mark of dedication.

Americans have not thought of themselves as a ritual people. The Protestants who settled the Atlantic shore and swept west with revivals, with few exceptions saw themselves as verbal types, impressed with literacy and the authority of the printed page. The founders of the republic, sometimes as Freemasons, consistently as Republicans, were to generate civil rites. Yet the Protestant and Enlightened leaders would have united and often did so against the "mere ritual" of Catholicism. Later Catholicism, without denying the Mass or ceremonies, came to accent dogma and morality.

The longer America endures, the more it rejoins the human race, the more it reckons itself to be a set of peoples who share tribal and religious impulses with "primitives" and the "world religions," the more at home it has become and will be with those who set precedents in the first European century in the New World. The Caribbean and Central American cathedrals and the southwestern American missions belong to pilgrims and tourists of many faiths. These bid fair to take their place alongside colonial meeting houses and capital domes as symbols of New World ritual impulses. After four centuries and more, they belong to everyone, but not least of all to those of Catholic heritage.

CHAPTER TWO

Add Two Traditions: 1608-1776

Coping

Coping became the basic need for the two new sets of people from Europe who spread Catholicism in the northern part of the New World. Of course, arrivals from Portugal and Spain also coped. Everyone does so in environments not fully of their choosing. Yet people remember the Spaniards chiefly as Conquistadores, swaggerers who triumphed grossly or failed magnificently. They were crusaders, plunderers, sure of themselves whether taking gold from Native Americans or sharing the faith with them.

Not so with the French and the English. Not that these Catholics came from nations whose leaders were any less sure of themselves than were the Spanish monarchs. Nor did they lack confidence about themselves and their missions, whether this meant planting colonies on earth or rescuing souls for heaven. It simply meant that they knew before they came or learned very soon after that their part of the New World was not conquerable.

The people already there might thin out through diseases, but basically they had to be lived with. What is more, these European explorers for a Northwest Passage to the Orient found a vast continent but no such passage. If they then decided to stay they did so on terms that forced them to endure a naturally harsh environment.

The story of the French who settled after 1608 occupies us first. They founded "New France" to match "New Spain" in the south and to cramp the eventually Protestant "New England" that was to lie between the two Catholic imperial outposts. France was not in a position, as Spain had been, to send large fleets to discover, explore, exploit, and settle western Atlantic shores. Her national development came later. European intrigues also kept France's monarchs busy. People who start second, as the French had to do, must work strenuously to catch up. The French did not work strenuously. King Francis I seemed quite half-hearted about New France. He seemed distracted, and could easily postpone or even forget about projects there.

A growing power like France, however, could not promote its European rivalries with Spain, England, or the Netherlands without also competing for access to Asia, a secure place on the seas, possible colonies in the New World, and, certainly, some of its wealth. In respect to the last of these, however, ecology and the environment worked against the French. They were northern people who, given Spain's southern head start, knew they had to go north in America.

Going north meant going to a forbidding climate. The first reports of those who sailed for French interests, Giovanni da Verrazano and Jacques Cartier, left no doubt about the severe winds and weather, the dangerous waters, the threat of inhabitants. Verrazano and his party sailed as privateers for Francis I, whose interests he served by raiding Spanish and sometimes

Portuguese ships. In a voyage begun in 1524 Verrazano sailed north from Carolinian waters and probably was the first European discoverer of what is today's New York harbor. Verrazano had a good eye for geography and landscape, and his reports were partly promising. In 1528 he sailed again, but never returned, perhaps having become a victim of Spaniards who would execute him as a pirate or of West Indies people who would kill him as an intruder.

Jacques Cartier it was who began to have to describe a climate that demanded so much. Cartier, Brittany-born, no doubt sailed west with expeditions of others once or twice before his own voyage of 1534, again for Francis I. He touched on areas around Newfoundland and the Maritime Provinces of Canada, taking the lands he encountered for France. Cartier penetrated as far as today's Montreal and Quebec. He included visual aids in his reports back home: he brought some American Indians along. While his Northwest Passage quest was a total failure, he had given birth to the possibility of a New France on the lands he claimed. His reports, published in 1545 helped successors know what was in store for them.

Successor Number One in importance and achievement was the much admired Samuel de Champlain. He was a religiously inspired adventurer who had sailed after 1598 for Spain. After a fur-trading expedition in 1603 in the company of other French commanders, he returned with his own party several years later. A royal geographer, he used all the opportunities for charting that these trips gave him. He knew what he wanted and where he wanted it: "Acadia" as a French colony and Quebec as its focus. It was in 1608, the most important date for French-America, that Champlain founded the permanent colony at Quebec. He discovered what is now Lake Champlain, a strategic body of water in New York.

Champlain became a colonizer. In 1610 he married a twelve-year-old and six years later brought her to Quebec. The couple was to separate, however, and his Helene Boulle Champlain entered a convent. In 1612 Champlain was granted the monopoly on fur trade, which was to be the decisive economic activity in a land that disclosed no Passage to the Orient. His later years were spent in exploration, land-claiming, investments, and an eventual governorship at Quebec, where he died on Christmas, 1635. By then the cast of New France had been well set. It was a cast that differed in most respects from those in New Spain to the south—except that Catholicism was to dominate in both. No later French colonial leader was to match Champlain for grandeur of personality, clarity of aims, or as contributor to a conflict that would be fateful for France down through the colonial wars with England in 1763 and long after for Canada itself.

Fate

The fatefulness resulted from a freak of Indian conflict and a single day's incident.

It happened that the Indians in what is now New York stood in the way of the French or anyone else who wanted to move into the interior. It happened, second, that positive relations with them were vital for anyone who wanted to engage in fur trade. Trapping left trappers alone, vulnerable, far from cities and thickly settled colonies. They needed peaceful neighbors and collaborators, allies against the elements and cooperators who could move fur along rivers and lakes and their trade routes.

It happened, third, that the Native Americans in these territories were constantly at war. They were skilled at its most cruel expressions, including torture. They were also quite sophisticated, like the Incas and Aztecs who play their own parts in the

Spanish conquest stories. Some were adept at making alliances. We know two sets of these peoples under the terms of their confederations as Huron and Iroquois. France, for reasons connected with 1608, found itself in partnership with the Huron, and thus, willy nilly, in enmity with Huron enemies. These foes were militarily superior Iroquois. The Iroquois became the constant enemies of the French and the allies of English and Dutch colonists who thus opposed the Huron and the French alike.

Champlain, like many other French pioneers, treated the Indians as being equals of sorts. He certainly knew that his companies could not cope without the aid of these talented, ingenious, and often severe people. Champlain matched others of the French in expressing curiosity about their spiritual outlook. Some interpreter must have been on the scene when Champlain talked with a chief named Anadabijou: "Then I said to him, since they believe in one God only, how had he brought them into the world, and whence had they come?" The chief responded by telling an Indian myth. Champlain countered with a narration of the Catholic's account of human origins according to the Book of Genesis. Such petite engagements under northern skies seemed to promise happier encounters than those that were associated with Spain, where it seems as if an impulse to smash everything was ever-present.

On a later trip Champlain had to decide on which dialogue partners to rely. As noted, he chose the Hurons and thus picked up as foes an array of Mohawk, Cayuga, Onondaga, Seneca, and Oneida tribes. Champlain was equipped with guns. The Indians, of course, were not. Guns were to be the determining factor in his relations. During an inevitable ensuing quarrel, his Huron guides, aware of what firearms did to promote their own security and superiority, relied on Champlain. He came through. First the

Frenchman noticed that the enemy, as he said, came "with a dignity and assurance which pleased me greatly, having three chiefs at their head." The Huron taunted. "When I saw [the other party] making a move to fire at us, I rested my musket against my cheek, and aimed directly at one of the three chiefs. With the same shot, two fell to the ground. . . ."

Now, "the Iroquois were greatly astonished that two men had been so quickly killed. . . . This caused great alarm among them." The alarm should have been Champlain's and New France's. A war, in effect, was begun and lost that day. The alliance and enmities would determine much of French life for decades, perhaps centuries to come. The Iroquois were resourceful and vengeful. They had found a worthy target for harassment and warlike acts.

What followed belongs chiefly to economic and military history, but it must be mentioned to frame the Catholic story. Whether priests and missioners or trappers and tradesmen, the French Catholics would always find themselves between warring sets of Indians, also around the Great Lakes and all down the Mississippi. Far from being the simple, peace-loving people of romantic dreams in Europe and equally romantic recall in contemporary America, the Native Americans fought over place and status. They also warred for ritual reasons and for the "hell of it." Anyone who wanted to save Indian souls or take their furs was inevitably to find a complicated scene. One needed courage to cope.

A New Age

French Catholics brought many assets. For one thing, France was undergoing its version of a religious revival just as Spain had been experiencing reform a century earlier. The French renewal was both mystical and intellectual. A fervent piety marked the life of lay and clerical leaders alike. This spirituality led not a few to want to evangelize, to share the faith and the warmth. At the same time, the life of the mind was being dedicated to new causes. The Jesuit order, so strong in France, was an agent of this. Making sense of Native American peoples, life, and worship were valid intellectual exercises. They had as their practical outcome some sort of access to natives who should be saved by faith in Jesus and the protection of Mary and the angels.

If Columbus and the friars were moved by certain millennial and even messianic pushes, the French Catholics also often came because of an impulsive philosophy of history. Call it apocalyptic. For five centuries some schools of Catholic thought had suggested that a New Age was being born. Now the apocalyptic types saw fulfillments in the discovery of America. Thus Henri de Levis, Viceroy of Canada, in 1627 became convinced during a period of intensity that he should encourage religious orders and charities to face "the evils of the age." The often secret groups of devotionalists included fervent souls who believed that these evils should be fought among Indians who were the devil's victims and agents. Thus, one Mother Marie de l'Incarnation wrote her spiritual counselor: "It happened that since my Religious profession, he held my spirit in a sweet contemplation of the ravishing beauties of his Law, and especially the connection between the old Law and the evangelical Law. . . . Now this put into my soul an extreme desire for the Apostolic life, and without regard to my stupidity, it seemed to me that what God was pouring into my heart was able to convert all who did not know him." Of the Canadian scene, she wrote, "I had not heard speak of the Mission, yet my spirit was in its desires in those strange lands." For ten years and more she readied herself to follow, and again she spoke of a vision that beckoned her to New France.

Soon there were women religious of her sort participating in colonial life. Thus the Hospital Nuns of the Holy Ghost were charged "to pass to New France to make the savages Christian or to remove them from barbarian habit to a proper and civil life," for these were "designs really filled with zeal and charity." Those who went would go "to reduce their infirmities, to participate in their ills and to sacrifice each day," in callings that brought them face to face with "horror and infection, wounds and ulcers." These were things "which surpass the natural" and would not be found in persons "if God did not inspire grace" and grant special strength.

Those who came did see themselves sharing in the New Age of the Church and the Spirit. They wanted also to see what Marie de l'Incarnation saw in the converts, "the fervour of the first Christians of the Church." The actual converts, for the most part, could not match this description, and hundreds of pages of Jesuit reports make that clear. Yet for the New Age in the New World it was important to be able to point to unmistakable signs that God and the French were effecting a new thing.

Because of tender and spirited reports like Mother Marie's and because it was not hard to look better than the Spanish and the English, the French had acquired a better press in respect to Indians. Most frequently quoted is the great anti-Catholic admirer of the missionaries, nineteenth-century historian Francis Parkman: "Spanish civilization crushed the Indian; English civilization scorned and neglected him; French civilization embraced and cherished him." As with all half-truths there remains the truth that makes the French case worthy of study and the half-falsehood that will not allow the French to get away with goodness. Apologists for the Indian find records of condescension and exploitation, indeed, killing. These mar the French record. Rather than spend even a moment defending the notion of French superiority, it seems better to point to their distinctives.

Scientia

Scientia: knowledge. The French wanted to "know" the Native American the way most Spaniards on the yon side of Las Casas and the hither side of a half-dozen Puritan missionaries did not. The Indians with whom French records deal were not members of a genus. They often are remembered by name and as particular characters. They made contributions for which they are known and should be recognized, insisted the diarists and letter writers. Behind the positive images was a background of French intellectual encounter that dated from the time the first Spanish reports started coming in. Whoever draws on the heritage of French Catholicism in American rootage almost inevitably is also drawn into this sphere where people thirst for knowledge. It could not always be an informed knowledge, since the reports were strained by the bias of those who wrote them and were read by biased Catholics who mentally rewrote whatever they encountered in these reports.

At the center of what was first known was a myth: that of the Noble Savage. This image began to take form in some Spanish accounts, but appears more clearly in French interpretations of those accounts. *Scientia,* knowledge, was also motivated by practical need. If one had to live with and cope with Indians and America, the coper did well to learn all that could be known from those who survived in the harsh climate and landscape. Yet there were also purer forms of intellectual inquiry. These were of the sort that the skeptical-minded Michel de Montaigne wrote. He was not a pure romantic, especially after he read Las Casas. He concluded with words that missionaries, no matter how well prepared they were, often learned existentially: "I perceive, that whosoever had undertaken them man to man, without odds of arms, of experience or of number, should have had as dangerous a war, or perhaps more, as any we see amongst us." And so it was.

The *Jesuit Relations*, annual reports that became equivalents of bestsellers back in France, were not random reports. They were calculated summaries, more or less scientific documents that outlined the details of Indian living. They were written by people who lived not between but with both extremes of the Noble Savage: innocence and cruelty. Often these sounded as if the Indians had no religion. Some of the earliest reporters suggested that one could start from scratch in dealing with natives. Just as often they reported on the most elaborate structures of ritual, myth, and institution. In the first case, Catholicism had to know what was not in America in order to bring something for the first time. In the second instance, Catholicism equally had to know what it was facing, for in New France there was no vacuum but instead a complex of often devilish, sometimes potentially angelic beliefs and practices. Champlain chose the former version. Here among hostile tribes were "brute beasts having neither faith nor law, living without God and religion." Many followed his view.

The Jesuits, however, were more sophisticated. These "Black Robes" came against a long background of coping and knowing. Pioneer Father Charles Lalemant spoke in 1627 for those who did discern among Indians a belief in the soul and the hereafter and some sort of divine creator. Their rites, however, did not strike him and many of his cohorts as being expressions of religion. A more formal report came from Thomas LeFebvre in 1650. It merits quoting: "Several of these people of Canada already believe that there is a God the Father, a Mother, an immortal soul, a son and Sun which is the author and preserver of all things, that the Father is above all, that since he has had to be stern with mankind the mother devours them but the son is good to them, preserves them and gives them life." Here seemed to be many possibilities for tying together Catholic and Indian religion. Some came across stories of a Great Deluge that, as if by natural knowledge, matched the Genesis account of a similar flood. Some reporters rejoiced to see certain tribes respond to the object and image of the cross. One Chrétien le Clercq pondered the origin of the cult of the Cross. He gave reasons that obliged him "to believe that the Cross had been venerated among these Barbarians before the first arrival of the French in this country." Certainly such people should be good prospects for conversion.

The issue confronting the Jesuits and others who "knew" something of Indian natural religion as the Spanish Jesuits seemed less to know, or at least to record, had long been called "adaptation." In missionary strategy, should one repudiate all that was present and start from scratch, but risk getting no hearing at all? Or should one risk totally disrupting people from their ways of life? Should one adapt, using whatever could be saved from native faith and rite and grafting new meanings and new names on the old? The French more than the Spanish and vastly more frequently than the English made an effort to relate by adaptation.

A Balance Sheet

For all the need to cope and to know, for all the mysticism and apocalypticism that inspired the mission, not much came of it. Huguenots and other Protestant critics observed the attempts at fusion during efforts at converting. They saw these as nothing but a laying bare of the ties between Catholicism and paganism itself. There were intellectual challenges which Jesuits at least had to accept. Some would call it relativism and include in that a sense of anthropological sophistication. Different rites for different folk seemed to be the pattern. While Jesuits were dedicated would-be converters, they went back home with or died with the knowledge that theirs was not the only way to produce virtues and that their right beliefs might often produce vices. Biblically they learned to blame Indian vices on the human Fall that the book of Genesis revealed to Catholics. Intellectually they began to speculate about how different environments colored different faiths. Such speculation also left the difficult question that adaptation began to pose: what to do about the places where the two sets of faith were so often parallel, similar, at least analogous?

Most telling were the failures, despite all the praying, adapting, and knowing. A community called Huronia did not work as a "mission" that would compare to those of Spanish style. For all the efforts to convert, inform, and discipline, never once did an Indian become a priest and very few women aspired to become nuns. Converts, uprooted from the practices they had known, often later reverted to them. Some totally lapsed and then became in some cases enemies of the missionaries who had taught and served them. When Jesuits or Recollects attempted to coerce Indians into belief they learned the grand lesson of North America: over the long pull, coercion could not work. Marie de l'Incarnation, for all her benign intentions, by 1660 was using the language of holy war and crusade to describe French Catholic strategy against resistant Iroquois. She wrote her son that she had come to agree with some frustrated priests "after so much useless effort and so many experiences of the perfidy of these infidels," that either Indians of that sort must be "exterminated, if it can be done," or "that all Christians and the

Christianity of Canada [will] perish. When there is no longer any Christianity or any Missionaries what hope will there be of their salvation? Only God by a very extraordinary miracle can put them on their way to heaven."

There was another side. When natives converted and the conversions were lasting, Jesuits in Canada and New York and then further in the interior lauded them as being devoted and charitable. Sometimes they even complained about overconversion among zealots who flagellated themselves or overdid penance and weeping on Good Friday and similar events in the church year.

Having given some account of the first martyrdoms among the Spanish it is not necessary for me to make extended entries into the annals of violence, heroism, and sainthood by elaborating on the better known cases of those among the Iroquois. The names of martyrs like Saint Isaac Jogues and St. John de Brébeuf are as familiar as any in colonial Catholic history. These were devoted and courageous missionaries. Jogues was even intrepid enough to spend a brief time among anti-Catholic New Yorkers and New Englanders during a time of escape and passage. De Brébeuf then returned to the Iroquois who tortured and killed him. Jogues was killed in 1646 by the Bear Clan at Ossernenon during a mission among the Mohawks, a tribe that often had been a friend to him.

If this is not the place for tributes to martyrs who endured great pain for their cause, it is the place for notice of at least one Native American of special sanctity. She was Kateri Tekakwitha, who is likely to be canonized. She was born in the village where Jogues lost his life. Her father was a Mohawk chief. As a four-year-old she suffered disfigurement during a smallpox outbreak that took most of her family. From the Jesuits she learned Christianity, but she had to sneak into the circle of faith because of her foster family's opposition. Finally her uncle, the chief, was notified that she would be instructed. He responded by turning her into a virtual slave in the household, and she had to be spirited away. She escaped to a Mohawk Christian village near Montreal. The rest of her life she devoted to prayer and suffering. Tekakwitha died in 1680, an exemplar of the faith the French would spread.

Scientia, the search for knowledge, marked many of the Jesuit and other French ventures in the West. There are countless accountings of topography, ethnography, and social relations in the *Jesuit Relations.* A typical case is that of Father Jacques Marquette, a Jesuit missionary who with Louis Joliet probed the Mississippi River. Of course, Marquette was a missionary. He took more delight in the baptism of a child along the way than in the many chartings that he performed or experiences with nature that he recorded. Yet the pursuit was also spurred by curiosity, by a thirst for knowledge. Did this great river proceed to the western sea, the Pacific Ocean? In 1668 Marquette worked among the Ottawas at Sault Sainte Marie, but he was restless, never fixed at a mission base. Five years later, in 1673, the two Frenchmen embarked on their paddling trip along Lake Michigan shores and then down the river ways that led to the Mississippi. After many encounters with Indians and some spiritual work Marquette grew weak from the exploring and died near today's Ludington, Michigan, in 1675.

One could continue such accounts by referring to René Robert Cavelier de LaSalle, another explorer familiar with the Mississippi and shaper of Louisiana. LaSalle was the first European to launch a ship on the Great Lakes and the first to lead fellow Europeans down to the Gulf of Mexico. Yet he fell victim to mutineers and was assassinated by them. To others was left the building of a Louisiana colony. There in 1718 New

Orleans was founded. One mark of Catholic intention and service was the opening of a boarding school by Ursuline sisters soon after.

Most of the story of Catholic New France belongs to Canadian, not United States history. France never had enough population to spare for New France's colonizing. New World population was therefore rather small. The Catholic fortunes in France had much to do with the fate of Canada and the French colonies. Thus in 1763 Catholic authorities in New Orleans banned the key people, the Jesuits. In 1773 the pope, as part of European intrigues and pacifications, banned the order itself. For years the best papal troops for the Spirit were off the scene and missions floundered. We shall meet the French soon again in battle with England, but the story of their mission can be bracketed for a time with a recall that they left outposts and missions in the heartland, as cities and towns by their names suggest: Vincennes and Dubuque, La Crosse and Eau Claire. These all announce that the French were here. They were the Catholics who paid attention to the personalities and practices of Native Americans. They adapted among them and often died for them, and by their hands. They remain models as copers and knowers, a practical people and one full of curiosity, whose record among native peoples was as mixed as everyone else's. Their monument is much of Canada and a special coloring in selective areas of Catholicism in the United States.

Tolerance   Tolerance seems to be a strange word to introduce the experience and achievement of Roman Catholics on the soil of the English in the New World. While, thanks to Iberian efforts, Catholics dominated in all Central and South America and the southernmost areas of the eventual United States, and thanks to France, through Canada and the northern interior, they were statistically a bare presence in the thirteen colonies that declared independence from England in 1776. The last thing the English Protestant majority would have credited Catholicism with is the theory or practice of tolerance. Yet no term indicates more memorably what transpired in Catholic Maryland in its beginnings or in New Netherland for a moment thereafter. Thereby, as one says, hangs a tale, and with it a need for thought about the concept of tolerance.

Two antecedent features of the Maryland and Middle Colony experiences demand expression. These were the intention of most colonists not to promote tolerance or religious liberty and the ferocious anti-Catholicism of the Protestant majority. This spirit mirrored the anti-Protestantism of New Spain and New France.

As to the former of these two, it is difficult now to do the kind of creative forgetting one must undertake in order to recall or reconstruct times when religious liberty of sorts was not taken for granted or provided for in the colonies of the future United States. Once a revolution has occurred, it can be very difficult to picture life before it. Americans may fight over details of religious liberty, usually under its later code name "separation of church and state." They may argue about the tax exemption of churches, tuition tax credits, crèches on courthouse lawns and the legality of "deprogramming" cult members. They may change the agenda for argument about religious differences in any decade. Yet these issues all deal with refinements of a basic principle. It was so accepted that by the late nineteenth century British ambassador James Lord Bryce could report with accuracy that Americans were united. They held "no two opinions" on the subject of the salutariness of their solution.

Given such a happy if often tense outcome to an ageless problem—how to relate God and Caesar, eternal and temporal—all kinds of Americans like to claim that it was their invention. Some religious groups have more claim than others. The notion, however, that democracy or republicanism with a distinct sphere for religion is a Christian invention only promotes the question: why did Christians wait so long? Modernity, new ideas, pluralism, practicality—all these had their parts to play. Still, many claimed that their foreparents came to America to promote religious freedom.

They did, but they wanted it chiefly for themselves. They wanted to set up outposts or colonies for their kind. People who believed otherwise than they had similar freedom—but should go elsewhere to act upon it. Rhode Island was all right for that in New England. Call it "Rogue's Island," though, said established Congregationalists. How could it be moral if there were more religions than one there, as the Baptists and even the heretical Quakers wanted to assure that there would be? Call it the *latrina* of New England, they said, since it had to take all the refuse. Whatever else the Puritan Congregationalists of New England and the Anglicans in Virginia were about it was not disestablishment in the nine or ten colonies where they could prevail. Anglicans came in 1607 and had their first Mass in Virginia. Puritans came in 1620 and 1630 to Plymouth and Massachusetts Bay. Religious freedom did not come with them.

The second prior understanding has to do with the nature of Catholic repute in these colonies. The last thing any Protestant there would have granted was a Catholic capability for tolerance. After the religious strife during the era of reform in England, after Henry VIII and Elizabeth I and especially after reversions to Catholicism and the persecutions by "Bloody Mary," Catholicism was seen as the devil's oppressor, not something that would allow space and freedom for anyone else. English author John Foxe's popularly named "Book of Martyrs" was a colonial bestseller. Its anguished prose and lurid woodcuts depicting Mary's victims, Christ's heroes, attracted avid readers. Isaac Jogues is known to have spent one day at Plymouth, but the fact that we know the name of one such stray only indicates how rare forays of his sort were. Otherwise, Catholics were people to keep out, to despise, to dismiss. Protestants named their own heroes in respect to religious freedom after centuries passed and the original partisans' passions had cooled. One was Roger Williams, a free spirit and dissenter who kept God and the state apart for millennial and purist reasons as a "Seeker." The other was William Penn, Quaker entrepreneur and visionary who founded Pennsylvania.

What a surprise, then, to read a sentence like this one summarizing colonial America in the most widely read and endorsed short work by the most noted of Catholic historians, John Tracy Ellis: "Thus did New York's Catholic governor [Thomas Dongan] join the honorable company of Roger Williams, Lord Baltimore, and William Penn as the chief promoters of religious freedom in colonial America." This sentence is early, vintage Ellis, from the days before Catholic John F. Kennedy became president of the United States. It antedates the Second Vatican Council in 1965 which passed a celebrated "Declaration on Religious Freedom." It recalls the days when even so generous-minded a man as Ellis was still obliged to prove that Catholics belonged in America and was pushed to use statistics to show why. The reader was supposed to think something like this: "There were 4,500,000 people in late colonial America, 20,000 or so Catholic. That means Protestants produce a promoter of religious freedom for every 2,225,000 citizens and Catholics for every 10,000—not a bad ratio."

Ellis was always too accurate to be countered on such points of fact. Dongan and Baltimore *do* deserve such mention, though whether that combination of two and two makes up the "chief promoters" foursome might be questioned. We need not deal with Dongan here at length. After the Dutch yielded New Netherland to the English, Irish-born Dongan was appointed governor by James, Duke of York, proprietor of that colony. In 1683 he convened a representative assembly which passed "A Charter of Liberties." Religious freedom was one of these. Six years later this capable governor had to flee his estate on Staten Island. He is remembered for that glorious moment of 1683. "No person or persons, which profess faith in God by Jesus Christ, shall at any time, be any ways molested, punished, disquieted, or called in question for any difference in opinion or matter of religious concernment, who do not actually disturb the civil peace of the Province. . . ." Mention of Dongan moves us ahead of the story, however, and blocks a more important set of figures named Calvert, titled Baltimore.

Twenty-seven years after the founding of Virginia and four after Massachusetts Bay, the Calverts settled a new colony, Maryland. George Calvert, Protestant-born, had picked a bad moment in England to become a convinced Roman Catholic, but convinced he must have been. He was neither a masochist looking for punishment nor a fool who could not have known his conversion would be inconveniencing. He did not fall wholly out of favor after the conversion, but he did have to resign a seat in Parliament and a secretaryship of state. King James I was benign enough to name him Baron Baltimore, which meant he gained an Irish title. Calvert remained a man of means and a dreamer who would found a colony. Through transactions too complex to detail here, he became proprietor of the land north of Virginia. He named it Mary after royalty, not after the Virgin.

George Calvert died and Cecil, his son, drew up the rules for the colony. In November of 1633 on the *Ark* and the *Dove* a mixed company of migrants sailed for Maryland. Mixed company: that begins to be the key. There would never be a way for Maryland to survive or attract as a pure and wholly Catholic domain. Others had to come, for many reasons, out of many motives, from numbers of faiths, and Baltimore knew it. Father Andrew White said the first Mass in Maryland in March, 1634. Here, under his cross, is the point at which many older histories of American Catholicism began.

Virginians were wary, and William Claiborne, Virginia's fervent anti-Catholic secretary, tried to wear down the Marylanders through raids and harassments. He once took White captive and sent him, in chains, back to England. Yet Virginia could do little more than express resentment. Catholics were also often problems to themselves and each other. The civil and commercial leaders vied with the Jesuits and other missionaries for land rights and over Indian policy and numerous prerogatives. Yet somehow the colony and its crops and trades and churches prospered.

The real troubles came from England, where the Puritan Revolution was making bad life worse for Catholics in overseas acts that eventually had to disrupt Maryland. The original charter of the colony was decisively but undenominationally Christian. It was wise for its drafters not to be specific because of the Protestant population under a Catholic proprietor. The plan was also no doubt part of Calvert's cunning, since he could not rely only on refugee Catholics. He needed Protestants to come and help invest and build.

In the scurrying for cover and the scuffling for place that went on as colonists adjusted to Puritan revolutionaries, Marylanders held an assembly meeting that passed "An Act Concerning

Religion," or "The Toleration Act." Half the assemblymen were Catholics, a fact that indicates more reasons to see the act as important. Its contents, it must be said, were less striking than its mere existence. But "the freemen have assented." Jews, of course, were not yet home free, though it might be said that Maryland seemed to grow in tolerance also toward them. The document lacked eloquence and was not epochal in character. It named severe penalties for blasphemers. The opening of the Act was characteristically—which means for its day and place, typically—crabby and cramping. Then, however, came the theme of toleration in a paragraph that Protestants consistently overlooked, while Catholics overlooked the one just before it— back when history was used mainly to claim all virtue on one's own side. The Act did not mean that Catholics had solved all the problems of religious liberty. It did mean that "freemen" could do their own thinking in new circumstances, and they did.

Tolerance, in any case, is not an alluring word, one that rouses strong passions today. Those who kill in the name of religion are interesting, while those who live and let live are dull. Tolerance, it is said in twentieth century times, is the belief of those who hold strongly no other beliefs. They can be relativists who honor other faiths because all faiths are held to lightly and their content matters little. Tolerance that merely acknowledges diversity and proceeds practically should make heroes of none who achieve it. Yet such comments begin at the wrong end of the scale. The Maryland Act appears against the background of an age which for over a thousand years had not been granting toleration. And it was not written only by people who held their own beliefs lightly. They had not thought through all the consequences of their outlook. They did not solve everything or intend to. They simply were beginning to fumble for articles of peace that would assure a free civil society. It still had some doctrinal limits, but it did guarantee the integrity of faiths to those who held them. Let the achievement be toasted, still!

Restriction

Restriction is an appropriate term to characterize the consequent life in the colonies. The Act of Toleration may have set a good precedent, but it did not solve all of Maryland's or Catholicism's problems. Three years later Puritans, a party then in power in England, seized it also in Maryland. Unhappy times for Catholics followed in the path of the intolerant. See, one says at once, toleration may be a weak virtue, but it is more valuable than the strong ones that replace it. Ask the spirits of Catholics past, Catholics plundered in Maryland after 1652. There were some persecutions. Catholics were kept from public office. Of course, toleration had to be repealed, its privileges revoked. Now Maryland began to resemble the England of a century earlier, as the domain changed from Catholic to non-Catholic hands. Baltimore was back again in 1657 and the old liberties also returned until 1691. That latter date was the time when Baltimorean proprietorship ended, Anglicanism became official, and Catholics were restricted. Catholics had to pay forty pounds of tobacco worth of levy each year to the Episcopal Church in which they did not believe, one that persecuted them.

Those were not days of religious fervor in Maryland. Catholicism had been making few gains when it was free and the Church of England made few when it became dominant. All through the 1690s the energies that might have been put into worship of God were turned into religious strife and the constriction of Catholic liberties. The Anglicans seemed to be getting ready for something bigger than the mere tobacco taxes. Year by year new restrictions came. In 1696 the law required attendance at Anglican worship, though England intervened on that retro-gressive measure. After the Glorious Revolution in 1688 the language of toleration was growing in English legal circles. The colonial policy of restriction would have been embarrassing. On neither side of the Atlantic were dissenters like Catholics yet assured full freedom. In 1699 a test oath was devised to keep Catholics from office. It derided some articles of their faith. When London passed an Act of Supremacy to assure the safety of an insecure crown, it also restricted Catholics. This meant a setback for the cause of tolerance in the colonies.

Then came the worst. Governor John Seymour, a man of mean spirit and profound hates, began policies that issued in what is remembered as the Penal Age. Priests were harassed and punished for carrying out their duties.

There were restrictions on immigration, even to the point that one would be fined for importing an Irish, and hence probably Catholic, servant. He or she might upset the popula-tion balance, now weighted so heavily toward Protestants. In 1716 a now incredible-sounding oath of abjuration came to be required for office holders and those who would inherit estates. Some Protestants could sense that these measures had gone too far. They worked to allow for at least private Catholic Masses. Now lay proprietors of estates also acquired new power in Catholic circles. They set up chapels in their homes and made the provisions for education.

Where was the threat? There were, according to the census, but 2,795 Catholics among the 34,000 Marylanders. All the colonial Catholics could be safely listed in the equivalent of a small town phone book. Yet, any free Catholics were too many for the John Seymours and others who had restrictive and anti-Toleration mentalities. Maryland Catholics had to use ingenuity and enterprise in order to endure and prosper. At

Bohemia Manor they built an academy. There the temporarily sequestered sons of propertied Catholics could be trained in the ways of faith and learning. Some families grew even wealthier. Charles Carroll of Annapolis was the wealthiest man in the colony.

This picture, with its glimmers of brightness, was itself shadowed by an event of 1713. Benedict Calvert—he might as well have been Benedict Arnold, thus bearing the name of another traitor, so far as Catholics were concerned—left the church in the hope of personal gain and proprietorship. He was soon rewarded with death, but his son, nominally now a Protestant, took over. The fifth Baron of Baltimore now was a turncoat Protestant proprietor who had no sympathy for Catholics. Apostates seldom have sympathy for those who know and represent their own spiritual past. Catholics adjusted again, however, and did not seem to know how to let religious restrictions limit them economically. Jesuits found ways to carry on work again, a sign that they were very clever or, more probably, that the oppressors were relaxed and inefficient. It was more important to have needling laws on the books than to have groveling or seething Catholic minorities who could no longer add to Maryland's prosperity. Better wear them down, non-Catholics seemed to reason, by letting them gradually defect through apathy or as matters of adjustments to policy than to persecute them back to passionate commitment.

In due course, events occurred to create distractions from the policies of the Penal Age in Maryland. Most notably, the colonial wars that reflected the nearly century-long (1689-1763) transatlantic battles between France and England broke out. Neither nation in Europe concentrated on the American stakes. The colonials were left partly to themselves and to the Indians to work things out. The last phase began with the "French and Indian War," an outbreak in 1755. It moved through the great

Plains of Abraham battle at Quebec to the peace tables and the Treaty of Paris in 1763.

All that belongs to military history, but the religious corol-laries and imports to it were patent. The thirteen colonies, including Maryland and Pennsylvania, which included a little spillover of Catholics, were overwhelmingly English. France and "its" Indians were the enemy and France, the enemies never tired of pointing out, was papist. Protestant evangelizers like the Reverend Samuel Davies could always accent their mustering sermons by calling this a holy war. Religion, however, had very little to do with it. For perspective, one might remember that thirteen years later the same preachers could be singing the praise of France, now their ally against England. Without benefit of allegiance to the pope, England now filled the role of anti-Christ. Religious symbols in wartime are eminently transferable.

Between 1763 and 1776 new alignments began to form. Through it all the Catholic Church somehow survived among the Catholic minority. Reports from priests and missionaries showed that most had long forgotten any original mandates they might have had to evangelize Indians. The colony was becoming largely English. It included thousands of slaves of the English, who were not Catholic. Restrictions from the Penal Age came to be relaxed and forgotten. Protestant neighbors found these cumber-some, unenforceable, and not created to match the realities they saw in their Catholic neighbors. They found something else.

Loyalty

Loyalty is the fourth mark of the Catholic venture that here deserves isolation. By 1776 war had broken out against England, a War of Independence that called colonists to make up their minds as to whose side to choose. On the principle that my

73

enemies' enemies are my friends, one could have expected Catholics to be loyal to England. Their Maryland neighbors were the ones who ordinarily restricted their freedom. Such was not the case.

There had to be compelling reasons in the American situation to impel such loyalty. While the Revolution was not a religious war, and while military leaders do not keep records of church participation, it is easy to go through that figurative phone book to see how Catholics lined up. Young men bearing the names Ignatius and Benedict and others that are not favored by Protestants were regularly on the militia rolls. Other surviving records show that Catholics more than did their part.

They had to work up enthusiasm on their own terms, and not because the "Patriots" spoke well of them as Catholics. One can prepare book-length anthologies, in fact, and have filled them with heated anti-Catholic comments by the would-be tolerant founders of the republic. Samuel Adams was a notorious Catholic-baiter in New England, where there were few Catholics to bait. John Adams, another man of Enlightenment reason and urbanity, was hardly more gentle. The mere report of a woman wearing a cross was enough to inspire suspicion of a papist takeover in a town. The merest hint that the Anglicans might try after 163 years to import or name their first bishop was all that it took to lead to a new degree of revolutionary fever. Benjamin Franklin, Thomas Jefferson, and other deists were nervous about revealed religion in general and about Catholicism most particularly. Only George Washington among the leaders promoted tolerance. He did so partly out of his desire for domestic peace and perhaps because of a genuine attempt to allow a live and let live policy to characterize the colonies whose armies he led. The Catholics were later to return the favors. They sent him warm greetings when he was elected president. It would have been hard for them to show such enthusiasm for any other founder.

If a sign of the cross or the threat of a bishop could help build war fever, the Quebec Act of 1774 inspired near panic. Parliament designed it in an effort to improve treaties dating from 1763. Quebec was to have jurisdiction north of the Ohio River and Catholicism in the west of the colonies was to be given full religious freedom. The whole proposal hurt American land speculators who wanted the west for themselves. It gave the colonists a sense of constriction: there, they feared, went their frontier. They united more than before against Parliament and the king.

Colonial leadership used the moment to try to woo support for independence-minded policies and actions in Canada. That meant dealing with Catholics, and putting a best Catholic foot forward. To that end a four-person committee including Franklin was sent to woo Canadians. They performed the mission with little chance of success. The one benefit in it all was the presence on the team, in a rare quasi-political role for him, of John Carroll. He was a prominent Marylander who would become the first bishop in American Catholicism.

War came, and peace after it. The Carrolls were important in both phases. Charles Carroll of Carrollton, John's distant relative, another wealthy Marylander, came back from French and British education before the war. He voiced early and at first tentative, then more bold, support for independence from England. A signer of the Declaration of Independence, Carroll was a strenuous backer of the patriots. He was loyal to the colonial cause, a visible giver of the lie to Protestants who expected Catholics to be loyalist to the wrong cause, on the wrong side. He had been on the mission to Canada with Franklin and cousin John. Charles Carroll earned the right to help draft the new Maryland constitution and often participated in office-holding. The first to sign the Declaration, he was the last of the signers to die, in 1832. It was natural for Maryland to choose him in 1901 to be the representative of that state in the United States Capitol's Statuary Hall. He symbolized the loyal Catholic population in the patriot and independence causes. If there had ever been reasons for suspicion of the Catholic role, the Carrolls should forever have dispelled them. They did not, as later chapters will show.

It became the fashion in later America for each minority group to show its credentials by citing the participations of its ancestors in the good things that happened in America. The War of Independence was the best thing. Just as all the major denominations sent greetings to the new President Washington, so the historians and apologists show that a cleric here answered the call to arms and one there mustered troups. This one tore up hymnals for cannon wadding and that one scourged the British.

Since the John F. Kennedy election and Vatican II, the realization of unquestioned maturity of Catholic political and cultural roles in America, such calling of attention has become at best gratuitous and at worst gauche. The task now is simply to tell the story. To make that story meaningful one must retrace steps to show how surprising it was to find Catholics among originators of tolerance or as participants in a republican revolution. It was equally surprising to find any of them surprised. The vast majority of them found American conditions favorable for faith and life. They liked it in Maryland and Pennsylvania and the colonies. They wanted to pursue their vocations, their family and church life—and then to welcome others who would come in their trail now, not to the colonies, but to the United States that took form after 1776.

CHAPTER THREE

The Republic: 1776-1852

Church and State

Republican values shaped the external life of the Catholic Church in the colonies that declared independence in 1776 and that constituted themselves a nation in 1789. These values may not have pervaded the internal life of the church. Many observers then and later noticed that. Yet as Catholicism came to find its identity, the internal life of the church ordinarily concerned only its members. They either acquiesced in the developing hierarchical model or they resented it and rebelled.

The external life refers to Catholicism's exposure to its environment, the image by which it was perceived, and the contact it had with non-Catholics and the nonreligious. This had more to do with determining the church's place than did its regular operations. The operations were usually treated as a "none of our business" element by the Protestant and unchurched majorities. Exceptions came when opponents of Catholicism pointed to its "undemocratic" way of running its own affairs. This indicated to them that it had no conception of what a republic could be. No one needed to take these charges too seriously. Protestants themselves invented a wide variety of denominational polities. The Baptists were extremely democratic and congregational. Methodists, their rivals, were extremely connectional and, in a way, hierarchical. Yet most citizens assumed that both were to belong equally in the Republic.

How Catholicism saw itself as belonging in the Republic and how it belonged became a preoccupying theme. Arguments in the 1980s about the role of bishops in shaping nuclear or economic policy or about the freedom of Catholics to vote for candidates who do not promise to work for legislation banning abortion seem new to many. Instead, they are based on perceptions formed as early as the period from 1776 to 1789 when the foundations of the nation took shape. Debates over whether a Catholic like Alfred E. Smith in 1928 or John F. Kennedy in 1960 would be free to serve the country as president without churchly interference were rooted in the controversies that went back to these foundations. Conflicts persist over whether "tuition tax credits" should be permitted to include Catholic scholars. These would benefit one particular creed and one church in particular. These debates often reflect uneasinesses and tensions that were addressed, often implicitly, by the American church's founders. Therefore any talk about Catholicism in its civil society has to begin with these beginnings—not in the courts of Isabella and Ferdinand, nor in the Gallican attitudes of French kings, bishops, and missionaries.

When one comes to this subject, the fashion is to speak of how Catholicism came to accept "the separation of church and state." That way of putting it is likely to remain current, thanks to the force of Thomas Jefferson's metaphor in 1802. He spoke too concretely of a "wall of separation between church and state." The United States Constitution knows nothing of such a phrase. James Madison, who played such an important part in shaping the Constitution, liked to speak of a line of distinction or separation between civil and religious authorities.

The Madisonian version makes more sense in a nation that never built a wall and whose citizens for the most part have not wanted one. They have overwhelmingly approved the tax exemption of properties used exclusively for religious purposes. They have for the most part assented to the use of public funds to pay chaplains in the legislatures and the military. They have given indications that they prefer what the Supreme Court with delicious paradox has called "wholesome neutrality" in relating government to religion. They evidently desire not a wholesome wholesomeness that would privilege religion or a religion, and not a neutral neutrality which would have meant creating a disability for individuals and groups that sought to give public expression to faith.

"Church and state" was also a problem-filled term in America because it reflected European ways of dealing with the issue. In Europe, normally, there was "the" church with which "the" state had to deal. On most European soil one church—Catholic, Anglican, Lutheran, Reformed—would be established and priv-ileged. Other believers, including often other Protestants on establishment Protestant soil, were limited, disabled, harassed, and sometimes persecuted, even to death. The state did the executing. In America there was no "the church," even where there were legal establishments, as there were indeed in nine or ten of the thirteen originating colonies. Those who supported establishment complained that so many "sectarians" were coming to nettle them. The sectarians, in turn, delighted in pointing to religious variety. They published huge catalogues of churches. As for the state, was it to be conceived as a local, colonial and then state, or federal, entity?

For the moment, despite all this, we can hold to the church and state distinction for Catholicism, because distinction and separation were particularly its problems. Professor John Murray Cuddihy has joined those who see modern life as chiefly a time of differentiation and specialization. These are complex terms for the modern "chopping up" of life into segments where there had earlier been organic wholeness. This chopping up represents a trauma to those who recall or dream of a primordial wholeness in life. Thus modern existence "chops" the bond between ethnicity and religion that Jews had known from immemorial times. In modern times alone people could write articles saying "Why I choose to be a Jew." Similarly, says Cuddihy, for Catholics the new word could be, "I happen to be a Catholic," a "happening," that signaled at least choice and possible casualness. In Europe, of course, one was a Catholic if one was born on, say, Spanish or Italian soil. Of course, religion should here be privileged. *Cuius regio eius religio* was the model and motto: the prince who ruled a region determined the religion of a region. You were either privileged in your faith or were a dissenter, an outsider on your own soil.

A republic that takes religious diversity seriously, as the United States was forced to do, as a free and modern state, could carry over little from Europe, but not even very much of the colonial legacy was of value in most states. Late in the eighteenth century Americans struggled with the realities of diversity and republicanism. The dissenters were coming to outnumber the establishmentarians. The philosophy of the Enlightenment, which most of the founding fathers cherished, was critical of "priestly" privilege. The act of getting the colonies to form a nation demanded that religion be addressed chiefly by being unaddressed. That is, the Constitution had to make history by being virtually silent about religion. The First Amendment which promoted religious freedom could not speak for the states. Not until the Fourteenth Amendment in Civil War times and after a Supreme Court decision of 1947 did the federal courts apply the First Amendment restrictions and freedoms to all states. The First Amendment simply said that the Congress should make no law respecting an establishment of religion or prohibiting the free exercise thereof.

"Simply said. . . ." An author who uses such a phrase for a complicated history needs to do some pinching of self. Events behind the shift were extremely complicated. Some republican-sounding people like George Washington and Patrick Henry could have lived very well with "multiple establishment." This meant governmental privilege and support for all respectable religion. Leaders of establishments like Congregationalism in Connecticut and Massachusetts hung on to at least mild legal privilege and tax support until 1819 and 1833. They were sure that order would break up and civility would break down if the state did not promote or favor their church and faith. The practical situation doomed them in the end.

How did Catholics do with "church" and "state," a subject with which they had thirteen centuries of experience? Their history on this subject went back to the time when Constantine and Theodosius helped the Roman Empire favor Christianity legally and then disfavor its pagan competitors soon after. Catholics had most at stake. There were those in Europe who began to monitor the activities of this upstart church in the New World to see how much it would push for its claims and acquiesce to others. The most difficult thing for Protestants to see after the middle of the nineteenth century was how little the Catholics said in the formative years.

The reasons for this were twofold. First, there was the well-known suspicion by the Protestant majority of all things Catholic. Their guard was up. Second, the Catholic minority was so small it almost should not have counted. We often project into the past statistical images gained from our own time. One can be impressed to hear early leaders of New Netherland, later New York, pondering how they should solve the issue of "church and state." Then we come up short to hear that the "church" of which they spoke numbered as few as two or three hundred people. No matter, as modern observers of the Unification Church or religious communes may know. It takes only a few thousand people to be highly visible on the American landscape. The Catholic Church in all thirteen colonies was not much larger in 1789 than was the Unification Church in the mid-1980s. Fewer than thirty thousand people belonged. Many of them were poor, illiterate, apathetic about religion. Yet they made up the representation of all things Catholic in their era.

Small this group may be, and bishopless it was; clerical leadership was necessarily all imported. There were no seminaries in English-speaking America. Those who came to lead the church, including some exiles from the French Revolution, had no background preparation to help them understand life in a republic. Many of them did not even know the languages in which they would have to minister. Lay leadership was even more meager. The few well-off and more literate Catholics had other preoccupations than deliberating on affairs of religion in a republic. Rome had to be of little help, since republicanism was not something with which it was familiar or which it favored.

Despite the improbable circumstances and sparse resources, the pressure on Catholicism was intense in a generally hostile environment. Somehow, however, the pioneers of the church in

America were successful as they adapted to the Republic. They used ways that, if they did not remove suspicion by outsiders, still left the insiders, the members, contented and at ease.

Republicanism   I have been using the term "republic" as if it is easily understood, its meanings agreed upon. In the present context it refers to what Father Thomas Gilby and John Courtney Murray insisted in the twentieth century that a republic was. They spoke of such a polity as a place where people were "locked in civil argument." Citizens were locked because they occupied the same landscape and were subject to the same constitution. No one was going to be able to ship anyone out, exterminate them, or utterly silence them. Their argument, therefore, had to be civil, which meant that it must deal with the *civitas*, the human city or public affairs. And it must be undertaken with some civil regard for the voice of others. The republic relied on argument. They based it on a very minimal consensus out of which could come disagreements and possible agreements. Republic did not mean agreement.

In further refinements, as the Republic took shape in America, it had to deal with pluralisms—of colonies turning into states, of religious and interest groups, and the like. No one was to be assured a legal monopoly. In definitions as old as those of Aristotle, as middle-aged as those of Johannes Althusius and as new as James Madison, a republic was *a communitas communitatum*, a community of subcommunities. *E pluribus unum* meant that out of many it was always in the process of becoming one. All this did not mean that a complete unity was possible or desirable. Unanimity would demand coercion and would not produce a republic any more than would a collection of human atoms acting utterly individually be a republic.

A republic sought unities and made room for individual freedom. But its politics was made up of interests, of what Madison called factions and parties and sects. They contended for and received power proportionate to their weight in the society. They achieved it through compromise. They had to make some sort of reasoned appeal to other interests. It was not enough to say "The Bible says!" or "The Pope says!" and hope for one's way among those who did not accept the revelation and authority or who perceived them in different ways.

All these were difficult ideas for Protestants who celebrated "the priesthood of all believers," for Puritans who believed in a "covenant" that gave laity great voice, and for Baptists who believed in soul liberty. Each of them would have finally liked to enjoy privilege. They had to be more difficult for Catholics, who lacked republican precedent and whose numbers were few. Yet Catholicism met the challenge, adjusted, and helped give shape to the republic. It did this so successfully that for the next two centuries almost to a person Catholics were puzzled by or resentful of charges that they did not really belong in America, that they did not understand a republic.

Through it all, European and, indeed, papal Catholicism seemed to go out of its way to make things difficult for the American Catholics. They gave the American faithful troubles in the eyes of their neighbors. Catholic historian Philip Hughes pointed out that at decisive moments the only place in the world where Catholicism on a large scale was free to live out its life exactly as it wanted was in America. Yet the pope was uneasy about republicanism and regularly said so. He was fighting virtual survival battles against European republican revolutionaries. They almost always were anticlerical and anti-Catholic. The achievement of American Catholic republicanism had to be almost entirely homegrown, from the time of

Bishop John Carroll to that of John Courtney Murray two centuries later.

Mention of Carroll comes as a flag to impel a return from essay to narrative history. The comments on republicanism may have seemed to be a diversion, an interruption of the story. Yet not to be clear about the background is to spread confusion about the achievement and the magnitude of what American Catholics effected. The career of Bishop John Carroll shows what needed to be done and reminds later readers of the people, sometimes one is tempted to say the person, who provided the cast for republican Catholicism. He promoted the integrity of the church in a pluralist society.

Carrollism

Carroll: the name seems to show up whenever one touches on early American Catholic history. In a community of 30,000 people, even in a day when most are college educated, it is still remarkable to find more than one or two memorable names. In late colonial Catholicism the 30,000 people were dispersed, largely rural, usually undereducated. To find three or more leaders in such a company is remarkable. To find three or more named Carroll is even more so. Charles we have met as the son of Charles Carroll of Annapolis and a founder of the nation. Daniel Carroll was another. He promoted the United States Constitution in Maryland, and religious toleration in the United States, which he felt should be a nation with a strong central government. This Carroll helped pick the site of Washington, which happened to include one of his farms. To show that one did not have to be an outsider as a Catholic: he was also chosen to set the cornerstone of the Capitol building in Washington in 1791. To have such lay members inscribed in a roll of honor would have been enough for the Carrolls. But Daniel also had this cousin John.

One is careful not to engage in hero worship or to subscribe simplistically to the "great man" school of historical understanding. People on page one of history books have easier times shaping policy and being remembered than do those on later pages. The competition for leadership then was lean. In today's world John Carroll might be one person among many. Since he has been elsewhere overpraised, there is a temptation now to engage in revisionism, to stake out a claim for originality. If everyone else thinks Carroll was special, why not gain a patent by claiming he was not so special? Most of all, pious Catholic chroniclers have regularly contended that Providence must have arranged for this man of the hour. Impious non-Catholics therefore should demand equal time and argue that the ways of Providence are too complex to be of any use in scholarly writing of history. There are plenty of ways to hedge bets, issue qualifications, cross fingers, and *still* find reason to make much of Carroll.

Even the bare outline of his career suggests reasons why one should reckon with him as the true founder of the Catholic Church in the new nation. He was born in Maryland in 1735. We have met him, a graduate of a college in Flanders and a European Jesuit-trained priest, interrupting pastoral ministry in 1776. He appeared there in the company of Benjamin Franklin and Charles Carroll trying to cement positive diplomatic relations with Canada as the War for Independence impended.

Politics in such overt forms did not suit Carroll. He was to make clear in his later career that it was an appropriate vocation for lay Catholics, not priests. The priest busied himself organizing the church, a task he took to with competence and flair. He seemed always aware that he was shaping a church not in a privileged Catholic society but as a minority in a republic that it was not likely to run. In 1783 he took the initiative with a small band of priests in setting forth regulations for Catholic life. He then made the move with them to ask Rome to appoint a superior for the church in the United States. His colleagues nominated Carroll. Pius VI gave him episcopal duties but not yet an episcopal title. It was 1789 before the pope listened to another petition and named Carroll bishop. He had won support by a 24 to 2 vote among the nominators.

A glance at his ecclesiastical career prepares me to take up the republican themes again. In 1791 at Baltimore Carroll held the first national synod. At that time he also began to plead for locally trained clergy. He was successful with French Sulpician help in setting up St. Mary's college and seminary. He fought off lay challenges to clerical leadership. In 1800 Carroll became the first bishop to confer orders on another, when he named Leonard Neale to be his coadjutor. In 1808, two years after he laid the cornerstone of Baltimore cathedral, where he presided, he became an archbishop. As Catholicism grew in size, geographical scope, and complexity, Carroll saw the need for new rules for governance and participation. In 1810 he and his suffragan bishops drafted some of these.

Carroll was coming to be the first in a line of exemplars among bishops as the pastoral administrator, American style. He did not write new chapters in the history of spirituality. There were no contributions to theology from his pen, except for some traces of a theology of republican Catholicism. This he did not get to develop, and his successors seemed generally unaware of it. He did have a vision of what a practical church should be in a free society, and used his skill to effect his generally benign ways. Carroll kept his vision of education. He added to St. Mary's as an educational base by encouraging the development of

Georgetown, the start of what later became a university. He encouraged numbers of orders of sisters to start schools for smaller children. His impetus lay behind many foundings of orphanages and other institutions of mercy. Later Catholicism took and takes all these for granted. Someone, however, had to promote them, and to assure that they would exist in a society where the state would do no funding and did not much care for the ventures. Carroll did. This he achieved while being nettled by vagrant priests from Europe, entrepreneurs who would set up shop independently of his kind of authority. He would be beleaguered by lay people who wanted to take the life of the church into their own hands. Carroll could be distracted by outsiders who thought his church did not belong in America. Yet he would not be remembered as he is had he only succeeded and triumphed in many of these encounters.

What we might call Carroll Catholicism derives from the genius with which he gave voice to the vague stirrings for responsible church life in the mixed republic. Sooner or later all assessments come down to that. Fortunately, his European education had brought him into contact with reasonable Enlightenment thought. He was well read in law. If republican church life meant being locked in civil argument, he was ready for it.

No lines of Carroll are quoted more frequently than his tone-setting ones: "If we have the wisdom and temper to preserve" the existing harmony between people of various religious persuasions, he argued, "America may come to exhibit a proof to the world, that general and equal toleration, by giving a free circulation to fair argument, is the most effectual method to bring all denominations of Christians to a unity of faith." Those lines could sound to Orthodox and Protestant Christians like a subtle public relations ploy that turns toward proselytizing.

If Catholics are nice to others and others are nice to Catholics, everyone will eventually find unity, which means, for a Catholic, that all will turn Catholic. Yet it is not necessary to see anything so grandiose or guileful as all that in his words. He was trying to figure out ways for Christians to get along, not how they should all tomorrow come to Rome. He was building on the Calverts' language of practical toleration and relating to the thought world of the Jeffersons and Madisons as they were moving it into policy. "We have all smarted heretofore under the lash of an established church, and shall therefore be on our guard against every approach towards it."

Would, could, later Catholicism remember this? Could Carroll's words mean what they said? Not until 1965 did official Catholicism go on record as saying that error had rights, and that all people had rights to express religious freedom. Much of papal and European Catholicism, as it fought defensive wars against radical republicanism throughout the nineteenth century, was devoted to implying or contending that the ideal state of the church took the forms of establishment and monopoly. The church could then only grudgingly and temporarily allow dissenters to dissent. Carroll is worth quoting in more detail. John Tracy Ellis has lifted up for all to see some lines the priest wrote in 1787 for the *Colombian Magazine:* "Thanks to genuine spirit and Christianity, the United States have banished intolerance from their system of government." They have often done justice to all denominations by "placing them on the same footing of citizenship, and conferring an equal right of participation in national privileges." The "mingled blood of Protestant and Catholic fellow citizens" had produced freedom and independence, and these would "now be enjoyed by all."

Carroll gave every sign of being able to live into his vision. Later Catholics, when challenged over their place in the nation, could well have cited him. Until the middle of the twentieth century they did so, however, with surprising infrequency. His writings and record were neglected, often forgotten, while he was remembered only for pioneering in churchly work. Much of what led Father John Courtney Murray into trouble in the 1950s, when he argued so openly for religious freedom and Catholic republicanism, was anticipated in Carroll.

It might have surprised Carroll to see himself remembered for this public aspect of his life. Most hours of most days had to go into regularizing priestly life and into determining codes by which Catholics would live. Though of Irish heritage, he thought it strategically wise for the American church to be as "English" as possible, thus to commend itself to an English environment. This was an increasingly difficult position to hold early in the nineteenth century. Then Irish immigration increased, Germans began to arrive, and the French wanted to continue to make their mark. The vision may not have been sufficiently expansive for the later immigrant church. Yet for its moment, it was strategically appropriate and did much to help Catholics get situated.

The father of the formal American Catholic order in the United States saw considerable growth, including Catholic missions in the opening West. He was able to talk the Sacred Congregation of Propaganda into letting American bishops take the oath of their office and orders without including a familiar European inclusion: that they should ferret out and oppose heretics. He found it difficult to stay in close contact with Rome late in his life when the pope was in effect in imprisonment in Rome. Carroll's attention then turned ever more to America on its own. A sign of his place was his invitation to speak at the cornerstone laying of the Washington Monument in 1815. He had to beg off for reasons of ill health, and death took him that year. The American Catholic Church is his monument. His argument for disestablished and nonimperial faith inside a pluralist republic is his special legacy.

Laity

Laity and their participation represented special possibilities and problems in New World Catholicism. From Christopher Columbus through Charles Carroll at both ends of the colonial era, it was clear that certain lay people were competent theorists and practitioners of faith for new settings. Through the half-century after Carroll, an impressive lay minority began to find its names in history books. This is remarkable because the pool of talent was small, the newcomers were largely poor immigrants, and means of education were meager. It is noteworthy also because for reasons of status, or because of mixed marriage, many prominent Catholics deserted the flock. They became Protestants in a climate where such church membership was convenient, even advantageous.

Were this a Catholic *Who's Who*, which it dare not become, it would include names with which to reckon. Some were major figures who, in later terms, "happened to be Catholic," but who because of their training, outlook, or dispositions made no contributions to Catholic expression. Here one thinks of Irish-born Commodore John Barry, active in naval affairs during the Revolution and in military shipbuilding after it. He gets named "the father of the American navy." Or one hears cited legal figures like Roger Taney, named Chief Justice of the United States Supreme Court by his friend Andrew Jackson. Religion did show up in Taney controversies. Some who opposed his appointment in 1836 complained that he prayed in his chambers before entering the court. Taney defended the practice and won his way, though his prayers did not produce for him a wholly positive reputation. A defender of states' rights who happened to be opposed to slavery, he let states' rights win out in his mind and boosted slavery in his notorious Dred Scott decision. This judgment found him opposed to citizenship rights for blacks. This ruling sent a slave back to slavery because states or territories, not federal government, were to determine policy.

Many of the traders and trappers who helped open the West were entrepreneurial Catholics, and some pioneers there became famed in administrative life. Thus John McLoughlin, who helped found outposts in Oregon territory after 1824, converted to Catholicism in 1842. A friend to Indians, missionaries, and newcomers, he was later beleaguered by some Methodist ministers who would deny his land claims because he was not yet a citizen when he made them. McLoughlin had been born Canadian and was not naturalized until after 1849. The opponents won. He lost property and power along with reputation. Yet as "the father of Oregon"—so many people get to be father of something or other in these expansive times!—he is remembered with the Oregon statue in the Capitol's Statuary Hall in Washington. The galleries of Catholic lay heroes also include Mathew Carey, Philadelphia printer and newspaper publisher after 1785. He was a pamphleteer and politician, a defender of things Irish and, especially in the War of 1812, a firebrand opponent of England. Carey's Catholicism was obvious and informing. His presence in lists like these confirms the scope of lay Catholic interests and the range of abilities. There is not much point in expanding the list; such elaborations usually come from self-defensive Catholics who have to prove that they belong, that they are achievers. We take for granted and can close that book now, having made the point: lay Catholics who could have run the church were available.

Lay running of the church was an idea that had come to many, an idea whose time seemed to be coming for the whole American church. Almost two centuries later lay talent is put to work in so many areas around and in the church. Still it occurs in the context in which bishops represent Corporations Sole. This makes them titular and even effective "owners" of church property. Yet it may be hard to repeal memory and picture a day when Catholics still had to determine how the church was to be administered. The experience of the church in China late in the twentieth century shows how difficult it is to conceive of a church run quite independently of Rome or hierarchical control. Yet some lay people in America conceived of their church thus. They set out to fight for their way.

"Trusteeism," or "lay trusteeism," is the code name by which the ensuing controversy gets entered into all the history books. When Catholics look for a usable past and set out to discern ways to enlarge lay roles it usually appears as the bogey. Be careful, one reads, lest "trusteeism" again rear its head and lay people get it into their heads that they will manage the property side of the church. Indeed, some lay controversy went even further than that, and moved beyond trustee concerns to the spiritual side of things. I am deliberately choosing not to detail that controversy here. Those who must revisit it for the sake of learning precedents good and bad are well served by historians who have written about it in all its complexity. The eyes of others glaze over if and when readers are taken on a city by city, parish by parish, movement by movement tour of lay trustee eruptions. More important here is to think about the reasons for the movement, the reasons for its ending, and the consequences of decisions related to it.

The Roman Catholic Church was by definition and design, to say nothing of habit, priestly and hierarchical in government.

How could anyone have deigned to turn its inner style into that of a republic ruled essentially by laity? There are several answers. For one thing, oldline lay leadership had been in North America since as early as 1634. It had gotten along with roving styles of missionary and priestly leadership and no on-scene bishops at all. This led the descendants of old stock to acquire liberal habits and a sense of their rights. They were learning much from their non-Catholic neighbors, a fact that could be listed as second in the sequence of reasons. Thus Southern Anglicanism went without a bishop from its beginnings in 1607. This freed lay landowners to run the church. They were largely unmindful of a neglectful supervising bishop of London three thousand miles away. They found ways to demean and box in the clergy, for example by refusing to tenure them. This kept priests off balance and relatively powerless, which is just how aggressive lay people wanted them to be. All this worked to lay advantage among such churches. Why not, then, in Catholicism, which needed priestly ordained people, but, it was argued, needed them for sacramental, not policy-making purposes?

The republican mentality also deserves to be cited here. If some acted on old precedent, others used new philosophy. The seal of the young United States includes the motto, *Novus Ordo Seculorum*. This was to be a new order of ages, in which people of reason could wipe slates clean and start over. It is hard for more weathered Catholics two centuries later to picture the context of an argument that lay people ought to be free to devise a new church appropriate for the new order.

Responsible Catholics also saw the success of lay-based Protestantism building an evangelical empire, forming its "errand of mercy." This included creation of benevolent and reform societies independent of financial support from the state. These Protestant remakers of the world were not anticlerical, but they proved that lay people sometimes knew more about fundraising and organization than most priests. They were not the inferiors to clergy when it came to devotion and faithfulness. Why not empower them in every parish to take command? In a republic, why should not the church be a republic?

Irresponsible Catholics, finally, complicated the picture. Some of these were clerics, virtual vagabonds who made their way from Europe as exiles disgraced, or simply in a spirit of personal enterprise. They had orders, so they thought they could sell themselves to lay people. Those who lived symbiotically off such clerics, including homegrown counterparts, were lay people who welcomed such "for sale" clerics—and then found ways to keep priests in their bought places. By no means did all of those who advocated lay trusteeism belong in this camp. Enough were there, however, to give credibility to priests and bishops who could shout "Chaos!" when the vagabonds and enterprisers made their case.

John Carroll and the other early bishops had to be emphatic about the demands and practices of appointing priests without episcopal authorization. Had the lay contenders won on this point, in polity and perhaps in more ways than that, Catholicism in America could have taken on a low-church Protestant guise and manner. The success of Protestantism, including its laic, mobile, congregationally autonomous Baptist forms, suggests that American Catholicism could have prospered. It would no longer, however, have been Roman Catholicism. It could not have been loyal, as the American church has so consistently been, to Rome and its traditions and policies.

The lay leaders were savvy enough to reach for alliance and protection beyond their own circles. This meant that they wanted civil government to help them. In New York they even succeeded in gaining passage of a "Putnam Bill" after an incident in Buffalo. Here was a flagrant passage over the line between civil and religious authority. The legislature decreed that lay ownership was to be assured, that clerics dared never hold title to church property. Not until the civil leaders needed Catholic cooperation in the Civil War, in 1863, did this encumbering but not often enforced bill see repeal.

In New York City, meanwhile, trusteeism moved further along than it did in Buffalo. St. Peter's Church was the original and persisting site of conflict. This had become a church of immigrants, impoverished people who could not well support it. Trustees filed for bankruptcy there in 1844. The trustees were stung by charges that they had been irresponsible. "Dagger John" Hughes, New York's very potent bishop, made these charges. It took a man as strong as he to insist successfully that they had to learn once and for all. They were not Protestants with a grass roots, bottom-up, lay to clerical polity. They were Catholics, and that meant top-down life.

Those who trace lay trustee conflicts usually come finally to the case of Holy Trinity in Philadelphia, where ethnic Germans wanted to run things. Or, symbolically down the street, to St. Mary's where issues came to a head. An Irish priest named William Hogan ministered there in the early 1820s. A cunning, ingratiating, and manipulative man, he made his way in Philadelphia circles and became an obvious threat by the way he and militant laity used each other. Bishop Henry Conwell had no choice but to risk the anger of moneyed leaders like Mathew Carey and suspend Hogan. The lay trustees reacted by drastic actions: Conwell was not free to come to this church, his own cathedral. Hogan was named pastor. Now Carey could see that they were going too far.

Conwell had to excommunicate Hogan in 1821. Now it was time to add an American chapter to the annals of schism which in the past had divided Christian from Jew and then East from West and then Protestant from Catholic. This time it came to be known as "the Hogan schism." In 1822 elections were held to determine winners between the factions. When the two factions could not agree to the other's choice, or even to agree to disagree, they began a riot. As in New York state during the Putnam Bill years, the civil authority sided with the lay radicals and Hogan. Pope Pius VII finally had to intervene. He forbade such kinds of lay activity. Hogan bowed but soon felt strong enough to issue a new challenge. Accounts of his subsequent career would glaze few eyes. With Hoganism repudiated, Hogan came to be known as a rake and profligate. He married twice, put some energies into running a circus and then departed from such straight and narrow ways to become a lawyer. He was appointed a United States consul in Cuba in 1843. Yet he is best remembered for having made his living as so many other vehemently "ex" priests did, as a speaker for and writer about anti-Catholic causes.

Not all disturbers of the peace possessed Hogan's charisma. Some of them had more capability for reasoned argument. In southern centers like Charleston and Norfolk, they used scholarly means to bring forth theses from classic Catholic sources. They supplemented these with American republican polity argument. They found some gifted if willful clerical backers and made progress for a time. Yet they were fighting Rome, tradition, the ghost of Hoganism, and an increasingly eloquent native clergy. They had to lose. Lay trusteeism and its correlate issues lived on into midcentury, but never gained canonical status or enduring victories. Lay people were free to pursue their vocations in the secular world and were asked to be obedient and loyal in the ecclesiastical one. They were to find countless ways to be more than passive servants of the clergy. They simply were not free to take over the canonical roles of the clergy which meant that, in such senses, American Catholicism remained a clerical body.

Mercy

The word mercy best characterizes the activities of Catholicism in the period before the Civil War. There are many elements that make up its acts of mercy. Some of them could serve as categories through which to address church life in those decades. A few of them demand separate notice.

Religious orders of sisters and brothers, along with priests, came to endure unimaginable hardships in order to spread the work of Christ and church. Franciscans, Jesuits, and Dominicans had been on the scene for centuries. They had explored the landscape and ministered to Native Americans and settling Spaniards, French and English people. The Sulpicians of France started seminary education and for some time dominated it. In 1797 the Augustinians established a province in Philadelphia. There were Capuchins in Pennsylvania and Trappists in Kentucky by Civil War times.

The new element in the national period, supplementing colonial era work by Ursulines at New Orleans, were the communities of sisters who volunteered to serve America. Then some sprang up here in order to minister in terms that they best understood to meet needs their founders best discerned. John Carroll supported a Carmelite convent in Maryland after 1790. In Georgetown, near where he had grown up, there were some Visitation sisters. These were contemplative, praying orders, setting spiritual styles to complement the usual picture of the American as an activist, practical earthbound organizer.

In Kentucky, Charles Nerinckx encouraged formation of the Sisters of Loretto. One can still capture some sense of the loneliness, community, and dedication by visiting the little cemetery at Nerinckx, near Bardstown. The gravestones there often mark the resting places of very young women who lived as Sisters of Loretto in very brief lives. Cholera and frontier diseases took them, but did not deter their sisters. They chose to be educators on the frontier. From Kentucky they worked their way west. Catherine Spalding helped found the Sisters of Charity of Nazareth also in Kentucky, which seemed to be especially rich soil for new orders. Spalding joined the order when it was but two months old and she a mere nineteen years. She became its first mother superior. Spalding set a precedent by stepping down from her role as a popular mother superior in order to encourage support of a rule that limited and passed around leadership. She never lost her influence or her mercy-giving impulses, as she served her sisters during a cholera outbreak in 1832 and when she helped found an orphanage at Louisville.

It is impossible to follow the trail of all these sisters. One notices a Third Order of Dominicans, which also took root in Kentucky, and the Religious of the Sacred Heart who settled in Missouri after 1818. There were Sisters of Charity of the Blessed Virgin and Sisters of Joseph and Sisters of Notre Dame de Namur and Sisters of . . . and Sisters of. . . . It seems heartless, almost cruel, just to run a catalogue of communities and orders without being free to stop to tell their stories. One must use the mind's eye to picture how in hundreds, and then thousands of homes, a dedicated young woman would be encouraged to enter the Lord's service, or discouraged from it to stay nearer hearth and marry and help produce a new family. One pictures the goodbyes, and the subsequent rare visits with families and friends; the shutting of convent doors, and the opening of these to send out the professed often by twos or in very small groups. From there they would take on physical danger in the face of epidemic or Indian attack. Or, worse, dangers to morale in their risk of utter loneliness, spiritual impoverishment, lack of fresh impulses for developing the mind, lack of social contact for people of rich personality.

The same mind's eye pictures the limits of these communities. Discipline was often harsh and hardly rational. Intellectual potential was often wasted on the enforced carrying out of menial tasks by the overequipped. Foolish penances diverted some from the immediate experience of divine Mercy. All those aspects are at the edges of diaries, letters, memoirs, biographies. They were all exploitable by Protestant enemies of those who professed such vocations. Those who despised and feared these communities fantasized about the possible sexual character of transactions that "must have" gone on behind convent doors where celibate nuns lost their virginity to rapacious priests. There was always a market for bestsellers like the at-once lurid and dreary *Awful Disclosures of Maria Monk,* the most notorious of the fake exposés.

The serious records show another, a warm and rich side to these communities. Sisters came to know and care for each other. Their lifelong intentions, based on sober vows, committed them not only to their Lord but to each other, until retirement would regather them from their disparate missions, since death would not part them. Relationships were nuanced. Friendships developed but were to be generalized, not rendered "special" or "particular," to the detriment of community or perspective. Most of all, in the rhythms of Mass attendance, hours of silent prayer, the performing of quiet tasks, and concentrating on missions of mercy and education, there was personal fulfillment. Now none were called to martyrdom, as the early friars and fathers in the southwest and northeast had been. Yet there was a sense that these agents lived on a horizon that left them particularly close to God. They served at home with another order of being, the divine. That divine impetus helped them bear pain, endure risk, simply endure. Are we romanticizing? The temptation is strong to do so. It has to be fought, especially by anyone who is realistic about human motives and the limits of action, who has a low threshold of boredom and a high taste for smelling hypocrisy. Yet having given all these hostages to suspicion, the reader of the record still has reason for awe. No, we decide, we are not romanticizing. If most of human history is suffering, says Theodor Adorno, to pass over history is to dishonor suffering; to ignore tradition and the past is to ignore the chance to endow past suffering with meaning; to be less than humane. We remember.

Saintliness

Sainthood and saintliness could be other headings for this period, for in it the first native-born or locally developed United States saints came to their vocations. Second of these, and first of the males, was John Nepomucene Neumann, who was Bohemian born and seminary trained. He chose to come to New York when he was ordained. Neumann linked up with the Redemptorists in 1840 and was the pioneer professor among them, having taken his vows two years later. He concentrated on Germans, who stood the risk of being neglected between the English and the Irish. His talents called him from frontier missions in Ohio and Pennsylvania to Baltimore and Philadelphia, where in 1852 he was named a bishop. A capable educator, he promoted parochial schools and saw to the founding of almost a hundred of these in his diocese. Neuman encouraged other religious orders in his diocese and when a group of black members of the Oblate Sisters of Baltimore were on the point of seeing their bonds and mission dissolved, he took them under wing and gave support. So impressed were those who benefited from his work that they began to speak in terms of saintliness and sainthood. In 1977 Pope Paul VI canonized him.

First honors on the American scroll, however, go to Elizabeth Bayley Seton, a convert from Protestantism. She was a widow who founded the Sisters of Charity. She could be considered the founder of those schools that Neumann so successfully promoted. She was the daughter of prominent Episcopalians and the spouse of a successful businessman. Content in the acts of mothering five children, she complemented her husband in New York social life. When hard times came to her spouse and his health disintegrated, the Setons moved briefly to Italy, where he died. A Leghorn family that befriended her in her loneliness modeled a positive Catholicism to her. In a day when such conversions toward Rome were rare for Americans she made the leap. Today such conversions hardly draw notice. In her time it would be comparable roughly to seeing a Jew turn Muslim in our own. A year after returning to New York, in 1805, she was baptized.

Efforts to support her children through teaching were not very successful. She could not draw on old friendships for support, but she did respond to a chance to go to Baltimore and open a school. Bishop John Carroll encouraged her announced resolve to start a teaching order. Mother Seton was the first superior of her foundation. From Emmitsburg, Maryland, where in 1809 her small order which included her devoted sister-in-law, started the first Catholic school, there issued many thousands more. Her Sisters of Charity, originating in 1813, is considered the first religious order invented in the United States. Seton was a doer who died young, at age forty-seven. By then she had piled up such a record of works of mercy and so exemplified an American model of sanctity that movements for recognizing her sainthood began early and endured. In 1975 Pope Paul VI named her the first United States-born saint.

There were sinners, too, and it would be cloying to over-concentrate on saintliness. Yet it would also be curt to pass over mention, at least, of French-born and educated Saint Rose Philippine Duchesne. Canonized (in 1988) for her work in America after 1818 as a Sacred Heart sister, her base was near St. Louis, at St. Charles and Florissant en route to a final focus at Sugar Creek, Kansas, among the Potawatomi Indians. This Native American work began, remarkably, when she was seventy-two years old. That was not a good time to begin learning Potawatomi but not a bad time to start serving the Indians.

Revivalism   Revivalism might be another way to suggest an element of a usable past to Catholics. Mention of the Redemptorists in connection with John Neumann provides the occasion. Revivalism, to most Catholics, is an embarrassingly Protestant, indeed, intrinsically embarrassing term. It is something that occurred along the sawdust trail or in big tabernacles or on fundamentalist television. Emotional conjurers in Protestantism who invented it induce the already super-religious to claim that they are Born Again, so that they can witness to others. The word connotes originally hillbilly and holy roller and later polyester and right-wing politics or prohibition of anything that might be fun.

Catholicism, meanwhile, it was presumed, was simply trans-mitted through the genes. Scholar Edmund Morgan said of the Puritan family that it was expected that godliness would simply pass through the loins of godly parents to godly children. Not so. In the modern and pluralist worlds, while religion was portable, the environment was often bewildering, hostile, or distracting. It did not encourage transmittal or grasp of faith. The pictures many held of highly pious and faithful Mass-attending Irish and Germans landing and disembarking from boat to nave of church were legendary, not based on fact.

Instead, people came from relaxed and nominal church life in Europe where everyone born to Catholic families on Catholic soil was baptized and thus considered to be Catholic whether they practiced or not. These immigrants found that both city and country life in America encouraged them to make a decision about their action. Their Protestant neighbors were doing so. They had to learn the same. For that activity, orders like the Redemptorists were born. Where once the pioneer had done mission work among Native Americans, now the successors had to do missionary work among the Irish, the Germans, the English, and other lapsed or would-be Catholics.

Historian Jay Dolan in *The Immigrant Church* and *Catholic Revivalism* has acquired a patent on the notion of appropriately applying the term "revivalism." How else explain the work of those who would come to a locale, announce a series of missions, preach emotional sermons, engage in fervent public prayer, testify, receive converts—or, more likely, enliven the lapsed who were allowing themselves to be heated up as Catholics for the first time? Dolan on page one of his book spotted the major Protestant evangelist Charles G. Finney having his eye on Clarence Walworth, a lawyer, convert, and priest, who was a successful preacher of parish missions. Walworth "has been for years laboring zealously to promote revivals of religion . . . holding protracted meetings; and, as he told me himself . . . trying to accomplish in the Roman Catholic Church what I was endeavoring to accomplish in the Protestant church." Finney observed that they had just as pleasant a conversation as if they had both been Protestants. "He said nothing of his peculiar views, but only that he was laboring among the Roman Catholics to promote revivals of religion."

Dolan gives credit to such priests as inventors, and quotes one from 1830 who said, "Everything is beginning from scratch," and "everything is just beginning to be built, raised, arranged, and maintained." People of such spirit could well improvise ways to reach sinners who led drab and guilty lives and give them emotional and spiritual excitement and the experience of grace. Like the Protestants, they also knew that the converts had to be sustained through small groups that promoted care. They had to have something to do. They built large churches and established parishes as enclaves to which immigrants could belong, where they could find identities, whence they could engage in acts of mercy. Theirs is a past now tardily being recovered. It could be that the modern Catholic charismatic movement and the recent episcopal injunctions to evangelize have been colored somewhat by Redemptorist, Jesuit, and other revivalist efforts. These were some of the more controversial yet helpful gifts or hints from the Protestant environment.

The West

Westwardness deserves to be entered into the record as an early nineteenth-century motion of the Catholic Church, a part of its impulse of mercy. This essay has to concentrate on what is new in each era. It cannot be said that what Nicholas Point and Pierre De Smet and their colleagues set out to do differed utterly in concept from what Jesuits and Franciscans were doing three hundred years earlier in New Mexico or two centuries earlier in Quebec. Yet awareness of that hardly licenses a complete neglect of such lonely heroes.

De Smet, for instance, or as more than a mere instance, was the premier ambassador to the Indians since Catholicism existed in the United States. He could live for seasons at a time in the northwest through more than 260,000 miles of travel and seldom see a white person. He could go rain-drenched, sun-baked, half-frozen with a saltless diet, lacking books and luxuries of all sorts; yet he seldom sounded self-pitying, and never wavered. The Belgian born Jesuit headed west from St. Louis in 1840, crossed the Rockies, and came to the Flatheads, who had invited him to the northwest. De Smet could stand between lines in warfare involving the Sioux and the United States and work among people on both sides, even serving as a negotiator for peace. He had Chief Sitting Bull's confidence, and found some successes dealing with him. Something of a hero beyond Catholicism, De Smet was a recruiter for his causes in Europe. Passed up for bishoprics, he stayed on the road until his death in 1873. No martyr, he may have known that the blood of the martyrs is the seed of the church, but he showed that some who stayed alive and served were also necessary for the church's full life.

De Smet was part of a movement that ranged the West from Bardstown, Kentucky, and Pittsburgh to California and Oregon. The lures of land and gold that called Catholics to the frontiers also impelled missioners, educators, and workers of mercy there. The West took on an almost theological significance, as it had for Protestants. Wisdom and revelation had always come from the East, but now God was to show new things in the development of the West. The story of foundings, of parishes, dioceses, missions, and orders, makes up much of the stuff of Catholic history. It remains a record of ingenuity and endurance which is told in hundreds of particular histories, several very long general ones, and by allusion and brief references in recallings like this.

Taking these all together, they do help spell "mercy" and the works thereof. To the simple Catholic, and at their best they were all simple, the earthly milieux were scenes for a drama whose real and final purpose was found in a background of divine and sacred activities. Through obedience to the hierarchy and to the laws and canons of the church and through belief in the dogma, through confession and participation in Mass and the sacramental life in general, and often through preaching and teaching, Catholics were to form a community of response that saw them as recipients of God's mercy in Christ. The least they could do was to pass this mercy on, first to their own, and then to those in need. The immigrant arrivals, the poor and ill, the uneducated, the lonely people on the frontier, all had needs that must be noticed and addressed. The day had not yet come when Catholicism on a vast scale could address issues of justice in society. They could protest injustices against themselves. They were, however, too few, too defensive, or too marginal in the beginning to propose ways to judge and reorganize society. That would come; for now, mercy would do.

Nativism

Nativism remains a topic hardly mentioned here except in reference to the awful *Awful Disclosures of Maria Monk*. Nativism recalls the mid-nineteenth-century efforts by Protestants to keep America Protestant, to try to exclude or harass Catholics, to use instruments and the rhetoric of hate to make life as miserable as possible for Catholics. Clearly, Nativism is a major subject and some understanding of it is necessary for any understanding of Catholic belonging and attitudes in America. Anti-Catholicism was endemic in all the Protestant settler groups. It existed among the enlightened and reasonable founding fathers, and among the unchurched. It was as old as 1607 and the first settlement and as new as the newest contact.

Now let me do something apparently perverse and risky. I am not going to make much of Nativism here. There are many reasons for that. They cannot include contentions that it is unimportant, its story unrevealing, or that it did not crest in these early national period decades. I hope they will not be seen as based on the fact that I as a non-Catholic do not want to own up to their grossness. Elsewhere I have written on Nativism in detail. One can also point to the very thorough treatments, like Ray Allen Billington's decisive *The Protestant Crusade.* As a Protestant I do not mean to trivialize the subject by quoting the late comicstrip character Pogo in respect to it: "We have faults which we have hardly used yet."

It would also be unfaithful to the record not to say that Nativism did much to form Catholic life. Whoever has suffered a momentary slight by an individual has to engage in great acts of imagination to picture what massive group slights to smaller groups mean. Catholics were sometimes deprived of livelihood, good name, dignity, and opportunity by Nativism. It was spiritually crippling, and worked as bad effects on the perpetrator as on the victim. There were even lives lost, particularly in a kind of ethnic warfare with the Irish and hostile neighbors in Philadelphia in 1844, just as there had been a convent burning near Boston ten years earlier.

There were ugly forms of literature, not only Maria Monk style, but also in the forms of *The Protestant,* a paper on which some malignant New York Protestants embarked in 1830. There were crass political movements and vile urgings of action against Jesuits presumably in disguise as jugglers, dancing-masters, or whatever, since they were invisible! To go on much longer is to dwell on a story that we do not here set out to do justice to.

Instead, without losing balance or permitting a sense of accuracy to slip away, one can point to neglected elements in the story. For example, think of how *little* bloodshed and destruction occurred. Here was happening one of the great population shifts of history. The white Anglo-Saxons, preoccupied with the race for the West themselves, were divided on lines of north and south, black and white. They were trying to make sense of an America they claimed to have built. In the midst of it all they also had to make sense of immigrants. These were, in the eyes of some, the heretical agents of the anti-Christ; in the minds of others, they were heirs of Bloody Mary and the Protestant burners. In the view of most, they obeyed a pope who hated republicanism. Yet the old majority had to make room for these aliens with all this on its mind—and did.

As dreary and horrific as the worst chapters are on American history pages, they have to be put into perspective. Weekly, Americans read of religio-ethnic-cultural-tribal warfare between people around the world, warfare issuing in riots, terrorism, open conflict. Such action takes more lives in two days than Nativist Protestantism took in two centuries. Telling the story of Nativism can easily be codified into cliché. It distracts from the story of the remarkable ways that Catholics and Protestants became neighbors and often spiritual kin who did acts of mercy for each other.

The best reason for setting the issue in perspective, however, is that it gained its prominence in an era when Catholics were still defensive. They had to explain why they were in America and what they were to achieve here. It was convenient then to explain Catholicism by reference to Protestant out-group pressure on the Roman in-group. That may well be too cheap an explanation. Of course, group bonding occurs when external agents apply pressure. Yet such an account takes away from the self-directed life of Catholics. The more one studies the record, the more vividly are made visible the ways in which most Catholics ignored Nativism as they set their agendas. They had work to do, and the best of them did not waste more time than necessary fighting the encircling Protestants and secularists. They could find positive reasons to be together and to work from there. They found these in their faith in God, their love for and obedience to the church, and the care of those close to them. Occasionally, for more than a few, they heard a call to heroism, sometimes to sainthood, and, most difficult of all, to the simple acts and words of mercy that made life endurable, that helped some conquer. They deserve better than to have their story told merely as being one of victimage by Nativists.

CHAPTER FOUR

Immigrant Peoples: 1852-1908

Newcomers Immigrants dominated the American Catholic Church in 1852 when the leader ship held its First Plenary Council in Baltimore. The opening of that sentence tells little. All the people, including the Native Americans who crossed a land bridge from Siberia to Alaska more than ten thousand years earlier, were immigrants. The issue of naming them such came about when the wrong numbers of people from the wrong nations came at the wrong time to the wrong places. A recall of what "wrongness" meant was made forever clear toward the middle of the twentieth century. Franklin Delano Roosevelt once addressed the old-stock Daughters of the American Revolution in paraphrase, "Fellow immigrants. . . ." It is the best known and least popular of any lines ever delivered to such a group.

The Roosevelt occasion is classic and memorable because in emotion and perception it pitted two peoples against each other.

One traced lineage back to colonial times. It gained credentials because its ancestry was involved in the Revolution. The members believed that they thereby were assured the right to name all later arrivals who lacked such credentials. The D.A.R., for instance, ruled out Jews even though Jewish women could also be daughters of American revolutionaries. Jews did not ordinarily get to do the naming.

Some Catholics did. It helped, for instance, if a Catholic traced lineage back to colonial Maryland and bore an English name. Such tracing licensed them to help set terms for later arrivals from Europe, even if these migrants were Catholic. Orestes Brownson, the century's best-known lay convert to the church, sounded anti-Irish when Emerald Isle masses began to arrive. They threatened to overwhelm the settled-in if doctrinally aggressive church Brownson had joined and which he now favored. Later on the Irish leadership, because it spoke English, was often nervous about granting "national" favors to Germans and other foreign-language speaking groups. In the eyes and the mouths of such hierarchs, Irish was no longer the sign of an ethnic group, but of a set of belongers.

In 1852, the year of the Plenary Council, twenty-six bishops and six archbishops flaunted Catholic symbolism and power and gloried in some statistics. The *Metropolitan Catholic Almanac* for that year counted 1,411 churches and 1,421 priests in 34 dioceses. The Catholic population was 1,600,000. That number may not sound large today; Chicago alone has far more than that in its archdiocese. Yet by mid-century this minority had become the largest single church body in largely Protestant America. The growth was only beginning. Many millions of immigrants arrived between 1852 and 1908, when the Congregation for the Propagation of the Faith determined that the American church was no longer a mission, but a church on its own.

Joseph Stalin once said that the death of one person is a tragedy, the death of a million is a statistic. With immigration, the uprooting of one is a story, the movement of millions is a statistic. If an author says 20,000,000 came the reader is inclined to respond with a mental "Hmmmm" or "Ohhh. . . ." There is no easy way to have a scale against which to measure movements of the past or, for that matter, the present.

One does better, then, to envision typical immigrant patterns. Picture a Catholic family in southwest Germany in the second decade of the nineteenth century. The family has happened to live in a part of Germany that must be shared with Lutheran and Reformed "evangelical" Protestants. Back in Reformation times and during the Thirty Years War, no one "won" this turf that would become part of imperial Germany in 1871. The family was not wholly inexperienced about living alongside people of other faiths.

Still, village life provided its shelter. The people were in walking distance from the parish church, and they personally knew everyone who attended Mass. The bells of that church marked their own hours of work and prayer. The family members may have been rather relaxed communicants. They remembered to make their confession only once a year. They attended Mass only a few times a year. Yet they and everyone they knew had their children baptized. They turned to church and priest for ageless, year-round, life-long services. This was home, and they liked it.

Then, one year, and another after it, disaster came. Winter lasted too long. The wells stayed frozen into May. The old stores of grain and other feed were gone. Cattle began to starve. Summer was too rainy, or stormy, or hail-filled, to permit crops to grow. The grapes were not nurtured by sun and did not ripen, so there was no new wine. In desperate times, plague piles upon plagues. Crop-destroying insects had their way, and mice ravaged the few leftover stores of food. There was no Social Security for the aged peasants. They had nothing, including no future. They had to leave.

With almost no funds, they were at the mercy of people who lured them away. Some migrated to Russia, and from there joined other German-Russians to America. Many went to Amsterdam and languished in that port. Without funds and prospects or, any longer, citizenship—they had to give it up as a condition for gaining papers to leave—they sometimes had to go back in disgrace, to poverty. Some made it to America. Before them, their grandparents had gone as "redemptionists." They were virtually slaves. They sold their futures and their children's, in order to get a new start. After some years they would buy back their freedom. They might begin to "make it" economically, sometimes so much so that they soon had need for other redemptionists to work their fields and home industries.

Roving these German villages were people who advertised the attractions of America. These rovers were sent by boosters for the new American cities. There was a need for manpower and muscle in them. Others came from western states which competed to fill up and become economically productive. America was advertised as a paradise of opportunity, something to which no place could ever live up. Yet after one uncle arrived, a nephew would come with his family. Then came cousins, brothers, and friends, with theirs.

These families took care of each other. A priest who spoke their language under a bishop who did not helped them form a parish. The leaders wisely talked them out of a penny a week. They used these to build great if gloomy churches. These reminded the parishioners of the Old Country. They attracted people from drab grey neighborhoods, and served, sometimes in almost competitive ways, as symbols of the group's "making it." Down the street in the same city there would be another parish with people from another part of Germany, or Ireland, or wherever.

Church performed many functions. It might inspire the people to carry on a mission. Soon another penny a week would help send a missioner to the Indian country in the West. In the church, the sisters exemplified a fulfilling way of life. Often a daughter would become a member of a religious order. Her vocation would inform the family about church doings. An especially bright son would find opportunity for education and service through the priesthood. Church was not only a place of worship. It became the place where one could establish credit and borrow and lend. There were picnics and dances. Often these occurred on Sunday, to the consternation of their English Protestant neighbors who thought everyone should observe a solemn Lord's Day solemnly, certainly without beer drinking and boisterousness.

On the Catholics' wall would be a crucifix. If they read, they could find devotional literature in their own languages. They resumed the response to the rhythms of the church year, the passages of life. Something of the Old Country came along with them. They missed people back home, but they wrote back letters praising the new place, inviting others to come. The immigrants liked it in America. They fulfilled all duties of citizenship. The last thing they could understand was why earlier-arriving peoples, not Catholic like they were, could not understand them, did not want them there.

This portrait may sound over-romantic. It does not include recall of the losers, who never made it to America or, having made it, who returned with weary hearts and empty pockets. It neglects the daughters who cried for their absent mothers, the women who entered bad marriages and were trapped for life among the ten children they birthed, life next to an alcoholic husband. It does not remember the probable majority that did not make the church a focus of community life or anything else. Yet it is a fair reminder of what many millions of Catholics did before and after the First Plenary Council to build up the Catholic Church.

The German picture is an almost luxurious one. The immigrants were by no means all victims of crop failure, disaster, or an economy that could make no room for them. Some came for opportunities, much as some young ambitious people from the American Rustbelt are today lured by the promises of the prospering Sunbelt. They probably experienced the same degree of satisfaction or dissatisfaction as do their present-day counterparts. Later some were to arrive in order to avoid unpopular military service, as in the case of the Franco-Prussian War in 1870-71. They were like the young men of America who in the 1960s fled to Canada or Sweden to evade the military draft and never received amnesty. Still others were inconvenienced by the *Kulturkampf*, a pretentious "battle for civilization" waged against Catholics in Bismarck's Germany after 1870. Religious visions, finally, inspired priests and brothers and nuns.

There were counterparts to many of these in Ireland, which supplied the largest number of Catholic immigrants through much of the century. When in the late 1840s the potato crop, on which Irish farmers had come to overdepend, failed in successive years there was starvation. To read the chronicles of deprivation in Ireland in that decade is to be confronted with a rare instance in which modern Europe, so far as famine and poverty are concerned, looks like modern Asia or Africa. The Irish poor had no choice but to leave, even if this meant being taken advantage of by unscrupulous "runners." These swindled the helpless during the transactions over tickets, stole baggage, or in other ways misused the migrants. In America the Irish were crowded into cities like New York, where they were victims of prejudice third only to that shown blacks and Indians.

The Irish even more than the Germans brought along or developed clergy and sisters who helped make the parish a center of life for families. They also began to learn the arts of organizing, taking part in politics, running the cities. The political machines they soon developed inspired horror in Protestant hearts. The old settlers saw themselves losing power to "teeming immigrant hordes." These immigrants were regularly portrayed as drunken, socialist and anarchist threats to stability and civility. In such portrayals, they were also seen as legates of a pope who had no use for American liberties. Yet the Irish endured, and eventually came to be one of the highest-income groups of all the ex-immigrant peoples.

After the Germans and the Irish, it was all downhill, so far as immigrant imagery in old-stock eyes was concerned. Later in the century the newcomers arrived from southern and eastern Europe, from Italy and the Ukraine and Poland. None of them spoke English and few seemed eager to learn it. Their costumes, menus, manners, and hopes seemed to differ too much from standard-brand Americanism to make them acceptable. Protestant liberals, people of humane and humanitarian bent, joined the ordinarily prejudiced people in seeing the city and the immigrant as the basic problems for the American future. The immigrants, of course, did not see themselves that way. They had a different vision of America. Of course, many returned to Europe, but most loved America on any set of terms. They preferred it to anywhere else. There were, to be sure, Irish riots in New York when Civil War military draft practices were seen as taking advantage of them. Yet the Catholic immigrant record in the Civil War was one of strong identification with either North or South, depending upon where one lived. This record was to serve the church and its people well.

Today Americans have much experience with what are called "ethnics" and ethnic concepts. In modern America some intellectuals, in their search for identity and their love of tradition, have recovered selective elements of their own peoples' past. They name their children after Old Country names. They add Old Country spices and herbs to their recipes. They visit graves and examine records in Europe to help them draw their family trees. Ethnicity in most cases is a part of charm. In 1852 or 1908 it was not called ethnicity and was not quaint or luxurious.

The most curious feature of the immigrant experience was the undifferentiated, "clumped together" ways that dominated Protestant impressions. While immigrant Jews, Lutherans, and Reformed, among others, suffered some stigma, one set of immigrants was most despised. These were the Catholics. Protestants monitored actions like the issuance of *Syllabus of Errors* in 1864. This was a laundry list of errors, a catalogue compiled for and by the potent Pius IX. They represented a form of rejecting the lures of modernity. Unfortunately for Americans in the tradition of John Carroll, the *Syllabus* condemned the republican way of life and criticized policies that granted religious freedom. Non-Catholics looked on again in 1870 when the First Vatican Council defined the infallibility of the pope. Such an action was seen as "inopportune" by many bishops. In fact, one of two negative votes was cast by the bishop of Little Rock, Arkansas, Edward Fitzgerald. The bishop revised his opinion with a "now I believe!" as he hurried to greet the pope in obedience after the count was revealed. How could one protect America from immigrants who took orders from someone who had, like the pope, opinions on "faith and morals" that conflicted with the

American way? To advance their cause and express their paranoia, it was advantageous for the non-Catholics to lump all Catholics together. The records find Protestants speaking of a "monolith," a "juggernaut," a "Jesuitical scheme" for taking over American politics and business.

Whoever knew Catholicism up close saw that nothing matched these descriptions. No one coordinated plans. The three nineteenth-century Plenary Councils were attempts to reduce chaos and confusion and to begin to bring order. Rivalries between powerful bishops like Baltimore's James Cardinal Gibbons and Rochester's Bernard John McQuaid or New York's Michael Corrigan turned into bitter and even legendary feuds. Protestants, however, treated them as all alike, all united, all one. There were some Catholics in management and vastly more in labor forces. Rural Catholics coexisted with urban Catholics. Most of all, there were ethnic Catholics.

Ethnic Catholics did not often know much about members of other Catholic ethnic groups. They did not always regard each other positively, as they fought for place in church and in the land. The most overlooked feature in most discussions of ethnic rivalry was the tension *within* immigrant groups. For one sample: around the turn of the century there were about 90,000 people of Polish background in Wisconsin. They were almost all Catholic. Their numbers in that state alone were larger than that of all but two handfuls of national Protestant groups. It happens that in the Polish communities of Madison, Green Bay, but most of all, Milwaukee, power battles occurred. They dealt with the shape of the city and the church. The common enemy usually was the German archbishop or the Irish hierarchy. It could also be a mysterious set of forces somewhere in America or probably in Rome. Anyone who would not let the Poles have Polish bishops was the enemy. Press and pulpit united in bringing the cause to

119

a head, but they divided over policy. Fighting within such a Catholic "ghetto" was more satisfying than fighting with outsiders. Later historians often write of the fact that a new Nativist organization, The American Protective Association, came to its prime in precisely those decades. They suggest that hostility gave the Catholic Church coherence. Not at all, or at least not very much for the people like Wisconsin's Poles. One can read the translated documents and histories of these "Polish Church Wars" through the seasons, through the decades, and never know that there was a Protestant in America or in the world.

There were, however, countersigns of common Catholic purpose. The church was not "nothing but" a collection of ethnic enclaves, European-based orders, and powermad bishops and politicos. Some new elements on the scene began to give a sense of common cause and purpose; they deserve attention.

Conversion

Converts, for example. Catholics once upon a time made their way through conquest. They fought and conquered barbarians and got their kings to accept baptism. America offered no such opportunity in the nineteenth century. The church was to grow chiefly by an ever more efficient and lively address to its own immigrant peoples. It succeeded in holding the loyalties of children in their large families. If there were accessions from the outside, these usually came through mixed marriages. Such unions were more rare than one might imagine. Social stigma from both religions' sides and the difficulties young people had making acquaintances across the boundaries of their Catholic and non-Catholic enclaves served as barriers. The third way for growth, then, had to be through conversions out of the non-Catholic population.

These conversions probably made little statistical difference. Turning Catholic voluntarily as an adult is a one-at-a-time, personal, often tortuous enterprise. It is not part of a mass movement. To this day most American Catholics can name a convert or three, but they cannot point to any mass movements, group conversions, or changes in the map of American religious forces, as a result of conversions. It was instead significant that a few very visible people came to be converts. Their acceptance of Catholicism, while it was personally inconveniencing and often led to ruptures of families and friendship, overall made the face of Catholicism more plausible even if more threatening to non-Catholics.

We have already met one celebrated convert, Mother Seton, now a saint. Another noted one was her nephew, James Roosevelt Bayley, whose maternal and middle name suggests other than Catholic background. He studied for the Episcopal priesthood after graduating from Amherst College, but in 1841 he left a parish and visited Rome. There he became a Catholic. Bayley returned after theological studies and was ordained in New York in 1844. He was an early leader of Fordham College and in 1853 became the first bishop of Newark, New Jersey.

Bayley, a busy type, brought a Protestant work ethic into his episcopacy. He founded Seton Hall College as well as Immaculate Conception Seminary. He made good use of religious orders, helping them start schools and institutions in his diocese. In 1872 he became archbishop of Baltimore, the most prestigious see, where he took under his wing Richmond's bishop and his own successor, James Gibbons.

Like many converts, Bayley was anything but a halfhearted Catholic. Students of conversion suggest that apostates, which are what people become to their old communities, bring special zeal to their new life. They have made choices, burned bridges, counted costs, suffered shame, thought things through, and they cannot go home again. Home has to be portrayed in negative terms. Apostates know where the skeletons lie in the old community. They can spend a lifetime taking revenge on their own spiritual past. Sometimes converts idealize the church as it was at the moment of conversion. They become very nervous or angry about subsequent changes made in it. Bayley, like many a convert, knew why he had become a Catholic. He knew what a firm one looked like, and that he wanted to be one. Meanwhile, his bloodline was also in his favor. He was not a new immigrant, but someone who had all the instincts and reflexes appropriate to a long-time American. It would be dangerous to make too much, however, of his high-level kind of transit. There were other kinds of odysseys, and we will look at two of them. They are those of the most celebrated lay and clerical converts in the century.

Orestes Brownson is the lay person. One hesitates to bring up his name, since he led such a varied, apparently fickle and sprawling life. His spiritual journey seemed so vagrant that it can hardly serve as anyone's model. Brownson was one of a kind, interesting in his idiosyncrasy. We wish to defend the thesis that conversion is *sui generis*, one of a kind, to each his or her own. What then can be learned from someone who borders on eccentricity, even if he has certain kinds of power? The question is valuable and demands answer, yet more than mere fascination draws us to a Brownson.

This particular convert reveals something about one style of relating to pluralism in America. To historians and social scientists, pluralism is one of the most interesting features, something to be noted and chronicled, pondered and analyzed. They can make it seem as if all citizens are equidistant from all spiritual options on a giant religious Sunday Brunch visit to a smorgasbord for the soul. Yet in practice not all Americans follow such a path. About 60% of those born in a religious group live their lives in it. If they make a move, it is often to a look-alike group through mixed marriage or through the simple accident of moving to a new locale. Most wandering Tennessee Southern Baptists are not lured to Hare Krishna groups. Most black Baptists are not teetering on the edge of High Anglican conversion. Brooklyn's Hasidic Jews do not get tempted by the Unification Church or Unitarianism. Yet America does have many alternatives. Most of them are aggressive and all of them at least implicitly invite and advertise. America has seen a type of spiritual sampler who eventually finds what he or she has been looking for. They settle in with enthusiasm, though not necessarily with a spirit of quietude and satisfaction. The pioneer and patron, though never patron saint, of such is Orestes Brownson.

He was born in 1803 in Vermont, the son of reasonably relaxed Congregationalists. After his father died, Orestes was fostered and cared for by neighbors through whose example he joined the Presbyterian Church. It turned out to be a mere pit-stop on his way. In 1824, after only two Presbyterian years, he turned Universalist. To keep the two-year cycle going, he was ordained in that scandalous church in 1826. It was scandalous because, despite its evangelical roots, it did not teach eternal damnation and thus seemed to be a threat to morality.

This time it took Brownson three years to move on, to the Owenite colony of agnostic communitarians. There as in Universalism he was an editor and agitator. He even helped promote a socialist-style party for workers. Of course, for them, too, he published. Spiritually still driven, he turned entrepreneur in 1831. Like thousands of countrymen and, sometimes, women, he started a religion of his own. That gave him no base, so he joined the Unitarian ministry in the 1830s. By 1836 he was back

123

for a more thought-out round with his own Society for Christian Union and Progress. This was again a one-man church. Brownson was ecumenical in his hates, for he despised Protestantism as he had Catholicism.

Down the road further for the New Englander was another new quasi-religious group, the Transcendentalists. They established Brook Farm, a high-class commune near Boston. Brownson favored this group and cherished its Over-Soul. This concept took the place of God or the gods and of the Spirit of Brownson's earlier years. Now his social conscience began to form, and he showed a gift for discernment. On a small scale he began to see what major aristocratic pessimists of his century like Alexis de Tocqueville from France or Jacob Burckhardt in Switzerland saw more clearly and on a vast landscape. They recognized the inhumane features of the new industrial order. They feared mass movements in the age of factories. Brownson became an embarrassment to his political allies in the Democratic Party for his extremism. He looked like a socialist petrel who could drive votes from the candidates he favored— including in 1840, Martin Van Buren.

In 1844 religious concerns seemed far behind as he established the journal with which he is associated in historians' recall, *Brownson's Quarterly Review*. Few Americans could have seemed further from Catholicism than this radical. Yet in 1844 he did turn Catholic, even though that turn was in every way to his immediate temporal disadvantage. He was a turncoat to all the groups to whom he had shown loyalty. He also looked like a good prospect to become an ex-Catholic. Why stop where he did in 1844 as a forty-one-year-old? He had decades to live and places to go.

Go places he did, but he chose to do so within Catholicism, which he wished he could keep as it was, or when it changed, to remake it. Brownson did not live at ease with the Irish immigrants who came in such numbers that they changed the church he had chosen to join. Pope and bishops could send him credentials and commendations, and did. On other days they must have wished he was not around. He feuded with bishops like "Dagger John" Hughes, New York's leader, who knew exactly where he wanted to carry the church.

Through the rest of his career Brownson showed unfailing loyalty to Catholic doctrine and his idea of the church and at the very least made its foes his foes. He kept turning out editorials and pamphlets to support such Catholicism, through the Civil War, through and beyond periods when his kind of argument for Catholic doctrine was not welcomed. By the time he died in 1876 he had come to be known as a thoughtful, moderately conservative writer on the United States Constitution. He was probably the most notable scholar of his times in American Catholicism, though his brusque and stormy manner was anything but scholarly. In a curious way Brownson had found repose, even though he seldom allowed himself to enjoy it and though he certainly would not let fellow Catholics turn complacent.

Associated with this erratic and jumpy spiritual Odysseus was a man of very different temperament and vocation, Isaac Hecker, the founder of the Paulist order. There are fewer mysteries about Hecker. Like Brownson, he published much and left many traces, so there is a kind of Hecker industry to match its scholarly counterpart among the Brownsonians. Again, Hecker was one of a kind, but he also bears observation since he pointed to features of America and Catholicism that continue to inform religious life.

Hecker, a New Yorker, born in 1819, also made his way to Brook Farm. It was the logical stopping point for the spiritually dissatisfied, intellectual searchers. The company he kept there included Brownson, Bronson Alcott, and the better known pathfinders like Ralph Waldo Emerson and Henry David Thoreau. "Forget historical Christianity" was the motto of some of these. They found the faith sterile, and numbing. Hecker did not find them so, because their journey was to be made without the land-marks of tradition and history that he found important. His short and direct road took him, partly under Brownson's tutelage, to Rome.

Hecker, like Bayley, immediately aspired to holy orders and was ordained in Belgium as a Redemptorist. This was the order that we have met on the frontier. It engaged in parish missions and revivalism with an interest in gaining converts and arousing the existing Catholics. The Redemptorist had a patent on missionary "bands," companies of evangelizers. The fact that Hecker's company was made up of five converts suggests that it fit this model. He and his colleagues came to be accomplished at their work. Hecker could have spent a good life among Germans and other new arrivals.

However, he was a man with a vision. Hecker's vision included the old-stock Americans who had anti-Catholic bias but spiritual hungers. He must reach them, since he knew them so well and had started life among them. People with vision do not always follow rules and regulations. Their calling does not always match the vision of their superiors. So it was with Hecker. He sailed for Rome and Redemptorist headquarters to gain permission to start the new work. The problem was, he had failed to get permission to come to ask for permission. He was ejected from the order by unthinking officials. Pope Pius IX evidently had to be involved in the case upon the appeal of such a visible and eloquent figure as Hecker. He let Hecker be released or dispensed from the vows he had taken among the Redemptorists and chartered him for new work. The visionary came back to the United States in 1858 with mandates for evangelizing and freedom to try to win converts, especially those that were not of Catholic immigrant populations. Three of his old fellow band-members joined him in forming the Paulists or, more formally, the Congregation of the Missionary Priests of St. Paul the Apostle.

Hecker still had three decades to live. He spent them strenuously, commending Catholicism to America and America to Catholics. Yet he was a man under strain who suffered nervous breakdowns. For one thing, he was a publisher and editor, notably of *The Catholic World*. This was an elite publication that is still consulted by historians who want to revisit judicious comment on the church of Hecker's era. Editors suffer deadline pressure. Second, he was a natural overworker. Third, he was a man on the boundary, as the most profound converts tend to be. He lived between old and new, between recall and vision. Hecker was also sometimes disabled by invalidism and had to turn work over to others.

Fellow Paulist Walter Elliott was typical of those who wore part of the Hecker mantle. Indeed, Hecker's preaching first attracted Elliot to the apostolate. For almost a half-century he was the main promoter of the mission of the Paulists. His invention was the Catholic Missionary Union. A prolific author, Elliott wrote a biography of his hero, Hecker. This book was mistranslated and malintroduced by an Abbé Felix Klein in France. Klein was an exuberant liberal who made Hecker sound too much like the Modernist that he was not. Modernism meant too much adaptation to the modern world. It was under suspicion by Rome. Elliott's biography of Hecker, then, despite Elliott's and Hecker's place in history on their own, found author and subject to be miscast contributors to charges that Americanism and Modernism would pervert the Roman Catholic Church in America.

A different aspect of Elliott's mission is of more interest here. Think, for a moment, of its delicacy. On the one hand, he was busy making Catholicism sound so at home in America that it would be attractive enough for people to want to convert to it. On the other, the act of writing thus forced him to make the church seem inoffensive, so at home that the reasons for joining it dissipated. While he and the Paulists set out to make converts, it was the less adapted and sometimes more belligerent Catholics, who portrayed Rome as an unchanging Rock, who won more converts. All this did not lessen the significance of the Paulist order. It only changed the direction to which leaders put their expertise. They formed "information" offices and worked in urban centers or on campuses in a mission that *did* commend Catholics to other Americans. This placed them strategically to be pioneers in the ecumenical era after 1962 and the opening of the Second Vatican Council.

Bayley, Brownson, and Hecker are unrepresentative chiefly because they are prominent. If 100,000 people "turn Catholic" in any year, only the celebrities among them get noticed beyond the parish and their family. Still, these are exemplars and should not be discriminated against simply because their names are known. One could add others. Notable women left a mark. Cornelia Connelley was an Episcopalian, wife of an Episcopalian priest. After the two became Catholics in 1836 the pope permitted them to separate in 1844. Her husband became a priest, Cornelia a nun. Tensions developed between them over their children. Her husband then left both the priesthood and Catholicism and tried to win them back in court. Abandoned, he lost a celebrated case and made his way back to Episcopal priesthood and away to Italy, where he died. Cornelia fulfilled her assignment in helping found the Society of the Holy Child Jesus in England. She had less impact than did the other converts on the land of her birth.

The Graymoor Friars of the Atonement was founded by the former Lewis T. Wattson, later Father Paul James Francis. At the end of this period in 1908 he founded the Church Unity Octave, celebrated widely in the ecumenical era. Wattson's conversion came in 1910, after his invention of the octave. The list of converts that Catholic historians like further to unroll includes politicians like Senator Robert A. Wagner, scientists like Samuel Haldeman, writers like Joel Chandler Harris, and any number of accomplished citizens. Such scrolls were important to Catholics in an era when they still had to prove that they were important, that they belonged in America. They were important for another purpose. They helped commend Catholicism to the American majority. Converts helped demonstrate that the church was not an exotic growth, an arcane and subversive institution—even if it looked ever more so to uncomprehending family members and friends of converts.

Nationalism

Nationalism, like conversion, helped minimize the weight of immigranthood on Catholic life in America. This did not mean that the immigrants were not nationalists. They were the prime ones. Suspect, they doubly proved their loyalty. Newcomers, they kissed the soil with a fervency of new converts, never taking the land for granted as would someone who spent a life from birth there. On the rise socially, they welcomed the society that gave them opportunity. Finding acceptance, they welcomed a form of government that generally protected them when local custom did not. Trained to be loyal, they were able to focus loyalty on the nation as well as on their church. Inheriting Christian traditions of militancy, they might love peace. They were, however, ready for war and they repeatedly were loyalist to military causes. To use a term from a later time, they were hawkish, even if American wars might be fought against

Catholic nations like Spain in 1898 or when Irish-Americans, with the Irish, might have found reasons not to be enthusiastic for Britain as an ally, as in the First World War.

The bishops were often gifted rhetoricians, zealots for nationalism. The late Dorothy Dohen made a virtual anthology out of some of their declarations during the nineteenth century. That language merits reproduction here as the best means to help latter-day citizens of a nation "under God" understand how they came to be that way. This means listening to Irish immigrant Bishop John England of Charleston, who died in 1842; John Hughes, whom we have already met in his New York setting, a strong leader who died in 1864; John Ireland, St. Paul's Americanist archbishop who died in 1918; Baltimore's Cardinal James Gibbons, who towered over the period; and to a more independent loyalist, Peoria's John Lancaster Spalding, the main founder of the Catholic University of America, who lived until 1916. Spalding alone seemed ready to offer some criticisms of the Catholic nationalism that came easily to his colleagues and millions of the faithful.

Most of these leaders were of Irish background. They brought or developed instincts like those that were long nurtured by Irish habit to combine the nation and the church in a spiritual whole, a holy cause. Certainly Protestant Nativism did its part in provoking nationalists to compete in "more American than thou" contests. Samuel F.B. Morse, the inventor of the telegraph and of literate anti-Catholicism, mounted a crusade to show that Catholics were un-American. He gave both Catholic Americanism and American Catholicism a target and a boost. Let it also be said that for Catholic leaders nettled by German or Italian and other ethnic "nationalisms," the popularity of the American myth and symbol served to help obscure the differences between contending immigrant groups.

The pressures led the more flamboyant bishops to claim that they, the suspect group, had actually been the inventors of religious freedom and the republican way of life. Such impulses help us explain these bishops' emotional references to San Marino. This was a republic so small that I will have few potential readers of San Marinoan ancestry to insult if I say that San Marino did not otherwise count for much in world history. It *did* count when bishops spoke. Listen to John England in 1826, requesting before Congress: "What was the religion of William Tell? He was a Roman Catholic. Look not only to the Swiss republics [which were very popular models in American Schoolbooks], but take San Marino—this little state, during centuries; the most splendid specimen of the purest democracy, and this democracy protected by our popes during these centuries. . . ."

Hughes also claimed that the monastery was the inventor of republicanism and that it should deserve credit. He, too, invoked the standard site: "Before Columbus . . there was one little republic [San Marino] installed in the Papal States. How long? For fourteen hundred years she has continued to preserve her liberty. . . ." America was "an enlargement of such a model." Cardinal Gibbons wanted Americans to recognize Catholicism as the founder of liberty. If they read history, Americans would learn "that no liberty which they possessed has come to them except through the agency of that religion which molded our barbarian ancestors into the civilized nations of Europe." Bishop Ireland: "The whole history of the Catholic Church is the record of the enfranchisement of the slave, the curbing of the tyranny of kings, the defense of the poor, of woman, of all the people." He went on: "The great theologians of the church laid the foundations of political democracy which today attains its perfect form" in emergent America.

131

Now it was also just as necessary to show that the American Catholic Church was truly American. This led some hierarchs to express fears of immigrants. Thus Ireland: "There is danger: we receive large accessions of Catholics from foreign countries. God witnesses that they are welcome." But their "affections and tastes" dared not "encrust themselves upon the church." He knew that "Americans have no longing for a church with a foreign aspect; they will not submit to its influence. Only institutions to the manor born prosper; exotics have but sickly forms." Typically Ireland could pay tribute: "America treats us well; the flag is our protection. Patriotism is a Catholic virtue. I would have Catholics be the first patriots in the land."

If Protestants at that time were sounding imperial and "chosen," so were the Catholics for whom Ireland spoke in 1905: "In the course of history Providence selects now one nation, now another to be the guide and the exemplar of humanity's progress." Today that had to be America, "the nation of the future! Need I name it? Your hearts quiver loving it." Again, "We cannot but believe that a singular mission is assigned to America, glorious for itself and beneficent to the whole race: the mission of bringing about a new social and political order. . . ." It all came to this head: "When I am asked: Do you put church before country, or country before church? I reply: I neither put church before country, nor country before church." They work, he said, in complementary spheres and are not in conflict.

Catholics in search of a usable past may not need more nationalism than the nation naturally feeds them. No one any longer suspects them of not belonging in America or realistically dreams of shipping them out. They may need some precedent for their critique of hypernationalism. That comes best from Spalding. In 1899 he expressed reservations: "There is a higher love than love of country—the love of truth, the love of justice, the love of righteousness." The true patriot would suffer rather than betray such causes for the nation. He criticized Manifest Destiny and wanted citizens to act with restraint when imperialism beckoned during the Spanish-American War. "Therefore we will not believe that the gaining of a few naval battles over a weak and unprepared foe had power to throw us into such enthusiasm or such madness as to turn us permanently from the principles and policies to which we owe our national existence, our life and liberty. . . ." Spalding was vastly outnumbered, but he was not unnecessary or without subsequent impact.

Building   Controversy vied with institution-building to provide the main themes for late nineteenth-century American Catholicism. To focus on conflict seems to do an injustice to the day-to-day life of Catholics. To neglect the builders, the layers of bricks, in order to turn attention to the throwers of bricks is somehow distorting. So one cannot well turn to the defining conflicts of the period without at least dwelling on some of the constructive efforts. Whether in immigrant-ethnic enclaves of Catholicism or in the kind that was more exposed to nation and nationalism, these provided organizations in which millions lived and to which those millions contributed.

Parochial schools serve as one example. American public schools were not born simply with Columbus or Independence. They gradually evolved and took semipermanent shape in the era of Horace Mann, around the 1840s—just when so many Catholic immigrants were first arriving. Mann was a Unitarian lawyer who knew that the schools could not be public or tax-supported *and* satisfying if they took on a sectarian character. This would mean a character in which he and other commissioners and superintendents themselves in any case did not believe. Yet they desired moral education. This meant that reflexively the schools took on the character of the environment. Spiritually it turned favorable toward a generalized Protestant ethos. Specifically, the King James Version of the Bible was to be read in the schools.

The textbooks, which are still available for examination, often revealed anti-Catholic and anti-immigrant comments. In such an environment, bishops like Hughes would wage warfare for equal rights and equal funds for Catholics. They could also lose battles, and did. All this gave impetus to the task of promoting parochial schools. These schools were negative institutions only insofar as they helped keep Protestant impulses at some distance. They were positive in that they helped make possible a Catholic passage to America that bred loyalty to and information about the church. The schools of this parochial sort were supposed to be normative and were prescribed to be used in every parish and by every family where possible.

By 1884 and the time of the Third Plenary Council, 40 percent of the parishes had been able to start such schools. In 1880 someone counted: 2,246 schools enrolled over 400,000 students. The follow-up reckoning in 1900 found 3,811 schools with over 850,000 students. In 1910 there would be 4,845 schools and almost a million and a quarter students. Most of these were elementary pupils, but secondary schools, more expensive ventures without tax support, were also making their way. A National Catholic Education Association was also invented to give shape to these.

Second, there were colleges and universities. No purpose is here served by listing alma maters in sufficient numbers to satisfy wearers of all old school ties. Yet the place of the sixty and more colleges at the end of this period demands mention. Spalding and others nurtured their controversial new Catholic University of America. It was born under strain because it was pontifical, which meant it was related to the papacy. It was also modern, devoted to the liberal education standards of the period. From humble beginnings under Father Edward Sorin at a Hoosier pond there had grown the promising University of Notre Dame du Lac at South Bend. The Jesuits founded Fordham and some Loyolas. Other education-minded orders were dotting the landscape with smaller colleges.

Later generations sometimes have mocked these schools for their failure to produce an intellectual elite to match that of Protestants. Of course, such criticism is in order. Catholics have been underrepresented until the present generation in circles of academic achievers. Their schools rarely matched the highest level of non-Catholic schools. Yet the carping judgments are often made without awareness of past contexts. These schools were restricted somewhat by the scrutiny of Rome, or of the European sponsors and founders. They lacked hard-won but still fragile traditions of academic freedom that the once-Protestant, still Protestant-related, and state schools were struggling to guarantee.

More important, one must understand the background of the constituencies. In the nineteenth century only a tiny minority of the generally better off Protestant population could afford to send its sons—rarely its daughters—to college or university. For Catholics, the dream was beyond the dreamers before there were G.I. Bills and governmentally-backed loans and endowed scholarships after 1945. Even the knowledge that there *should* be a dream was lacking in the more remote rural and the more crowded urban Catholic enclaves. Little wonder, then, that when the schools were first chartered, most of them—like most of their non-Catholic counterparts—concentrated more on simply passing on the approved knowledge and on teaching

135

useful skills than in basic research of a sort that luxurious Protestant and public universities were beginning to promote.

Institutions of mercy prospered. Orders of women in particular built hospitals and orphanages. The late nineteenth century has been described by Paul Starr as the period of "the transformation of American medicine." This scholar showed how in that period, when illness began to be treated outside the home and in proliferating hospitals, religious groups built places "to take care of their own." Others did not care for the neglected or they priced care out of their market. In due course, however, these Catholic agencies also served the general public. They remain a major point of contact between Catholics and the larger community.

Fraternal and sororal life was a fourth mode of building in these decades. The Knights of Columbus came to be best known after its founding in 1882. Many other kinds of Knights and women's auxiliaries and altar societies took shape. Most of these were highly patriotic organizations that provided life insurance, helped establish Catholic identity, nurtured group belonging, and provided entertainment. Most of all, these served like service clubs to help people pour energies into works of mercy.

Still more building went on among people who wanted to serve the mind and the soul of Catholics. Paul Messbarger has shown how pale and provincial was much of the literature of the Catholic guilds of writers. But the *Fiction with a Parochial Purpose*, as he called it, signaled something at least. It showed how leadership recognized the Catholic cravings for literature and entertainment, and began to build an audience and readership for work of better quality in the century to come. Some magazines, like the Paulists' *The Catholic World* or the Holy Cross Fathers' *Ave Maria* served important purposes in this respect.

What is now called a "devotional revolution" was occurring, in Ireland and in America. This revolution may have included artifacts that today would be dismissed as *Kitsch*. It prompted spiritual styles that look like superstition to the critical Catholic of later times. Yet it *was* a revolution of sorts, and was democratic in impulse. It recognized that not all were content with being spectators at the Mass. Not all were readers of history that talked about good old days when people once had known religious experience. Now, with churchly encouragement, people were to develop individual piety in their homes and private lives. Most of this worship would today be dismissed as rote and routine Latin repetitions, holding little esthetic appeal. Yet it also brought a sense of the transcendent, a feeling that one was on the horizon of another order of being. The letters and diaries of the period make that clear. The parish was a moral agency which promoted various causes like temperance, antiprostitution, and the proper bringing up of moral children. Liturgical reform and critical moral discourse would wait for a later time, but this does not mean that everything that went on lacked esthetical appeal or moral wisdom.

Conflict

Controversy, however, did dominate. The immigrants and old settlers were living ever closer to each other. The millions assured that Catholicism would remain to make its mark. The new moment came when it was necessary to define what that mark should be. Inevitably, Catholics came to fight with Catholics, as we have seen Wisconsin Polish people doing, or as we have heard that Gibbons *versus* Corrigan and McQuaid were doing.

One of the most fateful controversies had to do with the organization of labor. It may be difficult, decades later, to picture how long and hard, how century-long and very hard, it was for labor to win the right to organize. Americans then were still used to more intimate one-on-one employer and employee relations. Catholics, along with many other citizens, wanted to carry that model over into corporate life, where it did not so easily match. There, in the vagaries of factory and business life, the destinies of unprotected workers could be settled by fate and chance, or on the slightest whims. Fathers of families had no means to assure any part of their futures unless they organized. Catholics had much at stake because they made up much of the labor force in the new industrial cities and mill towns. Protestants in the middle class or on the farms carried long prejudices against the organization of labor. It seemed to defy natural law and American individualist ethos. Catholics experienced trouble both as they developed a middle class and because so much labor organization in Europe in the hands of radical socialists was anti-clerical and anti-Catholic.

In America the radicalism of the Marxists never gained much of a hearing, though it was to the advantage of enemies of labor to suggest that it did. Both because those who worked to organize labor might be fired, and in order to forge profound bonds, their early schemes involved secret societies or brotherhoods. To conservative Catholics all this looked like Masonry and meant a secret society that was anathema. In the eyes of others, it seemed such organizing was to be competitive with Catholicism where loyalties were concerned. In that instance as well as others, it had to be resisted.

By the 1880s the most powerful of these brotherhoods was the Knights of Labor, which was founded in 1869. Terence Powderly, who headed it, was a Catholic, as were more members than not. They took pains not to advocate violence, sound socialist or look radical. All that did them no good when there were outbreaks of labor troubles. These occurred in 1886 in the case of the anarchist-motivated Haymarket Square riot in Chicago.

Bayley, a man of rather aristocratic outlook, began to lead the opposition from his Baltimore see, but a Quebec Archbishop, Elzéar Taschereau, first made anti-Knighting into a crusade. He and other archconservatives were spoiling for a fight with Gibbons, who had succeeded Bayley at Baltimore and who was looking for gentler ways to deal with labor and the Knights. Gibbons may well have sensed that the secret organization was in decline. It was not worth making a target. It would soon be replaced by new styles of unions. The Cardinal did not need to sense, he *knew* that the membership was Catholic, loyal to the church, not eager to have to choose between faith and livelihood or lifestyle.

What to do? Gibbons, a genius at leadership—some see him as the most powerful and acceptable Catholic leader in the nation's history—acted as he often did. This meant that he did nothing, or as little as possible. He sometimes spoke of his approach as "masterful inactivity." When Taschereau saw to it that the Knights were condemned in Canada, Gibbons only took steps to see that the brotherhood was not similarly proscribed by United States Catholicism. Well, he did do *something*: he garnered ten *con* votes to two *pro* votes among the archbishops against such a measure in the United States. Gibbons and some colleagues also made pleas to Rome to prevent any persecution of the Knights. Their organization did dwindle. Their aspects of the problem were solved. By seeing to it that nothing happened, Gibbons saw to it that something happened: Catholic labor found the church not to be an enemy, which in that climate meant it was a friend. The European pattern was not to be followed in America.

Readers should be prepared for a second controversy, given what we have already said about ethnicity and rivalry. One Peter Paul Cahensly headed a Raphael Society that promoted Germanic consciousness and rights. A European, he began to attract a following in America. He visited German Catholic communities here and made connections with a Father Peter M. Abbelen, who was, not to our suprise by now, a Milwaukeean. Abbelen in 1886 took his grievances to Europe. He gained support there, a support which helped stir German communities to demand German priests, parishes, and bishops. Gibbons again stepped in, to stiff-arm Europeans who were in the way of the efficient ordering of the American Church. He urged that Catholics respect each other's heritages and form a United States-minded church on other than cumbersome and contentious national lines.

In a sense, both sides won. The Germans and others found their lineages honored, as on the occasion when Gibbons himself traveled to Milwaukee to make a conciliatory sermonic address. The policy of the hierarch was successful in preventing "Balkanized" or nationally chopped-up Catholicism from being established as a matter of policy. Cahenslyism as a formal movement lost.

Modernism was the code name for still another controversy. Sometimes this was blended in some eyes and ears and confused with Americanism. Modernism was essentially a European heresy that made its way in the circle of intellectuals, biblical critics and formal theologians, of which America had but few. The Modernists were generally well-intentioned figures who thought the church would lose the hearts of the faithful if it would lose their minds. They had confidence that the essential and eternal truths of Catholicism could survive change. They were sure that development and evolution should replace static views of the universe and could well serve people of scientific outlooks. Modernists came to be familiar with and were promoters of "scientific" biblical scholarship. This approach subjected biblical writings to the same kind of critical principles with which one would study any other document. Some of what Modernism stood for came eventually to be taken for granted among Catholic intellectuals. It must be said, however, that some of its European leaders did transgress the bounds of orthodoxy. They exiled themselves from the church or were seen almost universally to merit excommunication.

The Modernism that reached American shores was very moderate and always loyal. It was dedicated to help educated Catholics make the transit through a thought world that it was presumed must inevitably pass to another. The Modernists dominated only a few centers. They were rallied by the participation of Cardinal Gibbons at the World's Parliament of Religions at the World's Columbian Exposition. This was a World's Fair in Chicago in 1893. Gibbons there said a prayer and spoke circumspectly. The Apostolic Delegate Francesco Satolli on the spot saw nothing wrong with the proceedings. Indeed, Satolli seemed to give a blessing on the Parliament, on interfaith activities, and the American way of life. In due course, however, exuberant press misrepresentations and second thinking by Satolli, who was reached by conservatives with whom he was to side, were embarrassments to Gibbons and the progressive and Americanizing parties.

The progressives would have outlived their reputation and outlasted their enemies had the Parliament been the only issue. Antiprogressives, however, found many other experiments not to their liking. At Notre Dame Father John A. Zahm wrote on *Evolution and Dogma*. He was convinced that in the end there need be no conflict between the new science and the old doctrine. William Sullivan, a Paulist, spoke up for religious freedom and a new mentality appropriate to life in the Republic. Then, in frustration, he went over the hill to Unitarianism. Thus he proved to the intransigents that progressivism was on a slippery slope toward half-belief and then unbelief. At Dunwoodie seminary there was a nest of true, if cautious, Modernists, gathered there by Father James F. Driscoll. He encouraged publication of experimental articles in the *New York Review*, a journal that issued from that school. The Vatican, through the Apostolic Delegate, kept its eye on the *Review* and on Driscoll, and eventually alerted the archbishop who applied pressure against Dunwoodie. The *Review* quietly folded, pleading loss of funds. The conclave of promising scholars disbanded.

If the catalyst for the attack on Americanism was the publication of Klein's version of Hecker's biography, incidents in Europe also led to the condemnation of Modernism, even in its mild and tentative American forms. In 1907 Pius X listed a new pair of syllabi of errors and in a decree, *Lamentabili Sane Exitu*, and an encyclical, *Pascendi Dominici Gregis*, issued condemnations of anything that looked Modernist. For a half-century Catholic intellectuals in America were forced to play it safe. They played it thus even if the pope named no names in the United States and would have had to look closely to find anything there bordering on heresy.

The pathos—indeed, the tragedy of these actions—was that they took in too much and were too usable by people who could henceforth work to stifle theological statement. Catholic energies went elsewhere. The church's open encounter with the thought of the times had to wait almost until the Second Vatican Council.

Despite all these conflicts, the church emerged from the years of its formation as an immigrant body intact, growing, and strong. In 1908 the Vatican took this American church out from under the care of the Congregation de Propaganda Fide. There were few, if any, reasons to be suspicious of this loyal and prospering expression of Catholicism.

Public Catholicism: 1908-1960

Background   Public or social Catholicism in America was a turn-of-the-century invention that matured through the decades which followed. To invent means both to discover and to make up. "Invention" here means both that Catholics found resources to meet social change in America and that they made up new ways to meet the new situations of public life in an industrial world.

Some Catholics and many mass communicators may be surprised at this dating of the origins of the movement. They often leave the impression that when the bishops in the mid-1980s, for example, began to issue pastoral letters on nuclear armament and the economy they were breaking precedent and starting something new. Not at all. They belonged to a long lineage. Other Catholics plus some historians and theologians from beyond their church may be surprised for other reasons. They would say that social Catholicism was not a turn-of-the-century invention. Instead it belonged to a heritage of first-century

Christianity. It has its roots in the ministry of Jesus, the agency of the early church, and the writings of St. Paul. In this way of looking, it is social Catholicism that provides the norms. To adapt Catholic teachings in order to make them match the terms of classical laissez-faire economics, competitive individualism, and American capitalism was the new and difficult invention. What Catholics who cherish these latter terms have done, it is then said, is to have twisted and corrupted the standard Catholic teaching and practice of the ages.

Given such opposing perceptions which show up so regularly in controversy and reports on Catholicism in public life, it becomes necessary to define what social Catholicism here means, and then to point to its rootage. By social Catholicism we refer to the Catholic Church's analogues to the Protestant social gospel and to many and varied continental and British social Christian movements. Catholic or not, they grew up on Christian soil. Their leaders addressed issues of justice and equity in the complex world that emerged a century into the Industrial Revolution.

Social Catholicism set out to do in the sphere of justice what the Catholicism of the previous century set out to address through errands and agencies of mercy. Not that these mercy-giving efforts were no longer needed or that support of them declined. Anything but that. Yet in the eyes of Catholic social agents, the old forms were inadequate. The admirable attempts to build orphanages, provide charity kitchens, house people who had no home, reform individual alcoholics or prostitutes, provide free if minimal medical care—these were all too minor and too partial. They were too focused on a single individual victim to be of much good in respect to grave societal problems.

Social Catholicism, instead, argued that the church must help get to the root of these problems. It must do so by recovering first of all a sense of its own corporate character. The church was the mystical body of Christ. The members, responsive to the magisterial teaching and the hierarchial administration, were parts of that body the way fingers and arms and legs are part of a physical body. Practically, this meant that the church must make some corporate addresses to social problems. It must bring its common resources together in order to effect change in society.

When Catholicism discovered and countered the structural and institutional forms of injustice, this did not mean that souls would be saved, sad hearts made glad, heaven filled, or the church's work completed. Most agents of social Catholicism were perfectly orthodox about the doctrinal teachings and the work of the church in respect to the need for sinners to be saved. They were often themselves people of personal piety. They came to be known as especially faithful to the doctrines of the church even where these were not "up front." They simply felt that the church must precede, surround, and follow its soul-saving activity with a mission of care in which justice and mercy met together.

For social Catholicism this insight began with an attempt to teach and convince the faithful themselves of their responsibility to be just. Second, it sometimes meant attempts to change the hearts of other religious people, so that they might follow the teachings on social justice in their own traditions. This assumption was often muted in formal statements before the Second Vatican Council. With only a few exceptions, there were no contacts across religious bounds. The Catholic Church did not have much hope of influencing Protestants and Jews.

The Catholic leadership also addressed the citizens at large and their legislatures. Catholicism in its official teachings and policies was more interested in making unjust acts unthinkable than in merely making them illegal. Hearts might not change, however, as fast as needs presented themselves. This meant, for example, that social Catholicism often worked to have mediators present when labor and management met in crisis. It worked to have Congress and state legislatures pass laws assuring "a living wage," restricting child labor, or protecting the rights of laborers to organize. For this reason, the church cultivated its members who were active in politics. Chancery offices and city halls were often in touch. Especially in cities where Catholics were huge voting blocs, politics had to take their interests into consideration. Catholic leaders insisted, however, that theirs was not simply a self-protective interest on behalf of a church membership that was often lower class, its men active in labor movements. They were, they insisted, concerned with all God's children, Catholic or not.

The invention of social Catholicism in the United States occurred against the background of European change during the nineteenth century. In most European states there was little separation of church and state. This meant the absence of a thoroughly voluntary pattern in which the church must persuade citizens to act in certain ways. Catholic social leaders from Pope Leo XIII on down, were learning that they must also persuade people. So were bishops in the English and Irish Church. They began to counter intemperance in the use of alcoholic beverages. They wanted to limit the way liquor interests exploited wage-earners. These interests often encouraged heads of families into addiction and slavery to drink, thus impoverishing them and victimizing their families.

The work of Félicité Robert de Lamennais, who died in 1854, typified the delicate mission of agents of the new in Europe. With considerable insight and literary flair he discerned and spoke to the situation of industrial workers. He immediately found himself confronting interests that opposed such "meddling." Lamennais found that he needed a lever against

146

corrupt French policies and figures in church and state. He found these in papal teachings, with which he agreed. He began to assert support of these and to appeal to them in such radically ultramontane ways that he became an embarrassment to the pope. He was eventually condemned. Lamennais died outside the church as a son who, many said, saw too soon what others have not seen as yet.

In Germany, Wilhelm Emmanuel Ketteler, the bishop of Mainz, was a pioneer. He had to work by means of persuasion as he spent his life trying to extricate the church from the tangles of a dominating state. In 1864 Ketteler published a major book on the church and the question of the industrial worker, whom he championed in the framework of Catholic orthodoxy. The bishop had counterparts in England and in America, leaders who took great pains to use the tradition and the new papal statements. He combined these with social passion and alliances with leaders who also saw the problems of such workers.

A third European became far more important for American social Catholicism. He was a far safer choice as model, a far more potent name to invoke. Pope Leo XIII, being pope, could hardly be described as marginal in Catholicism or of uncertain status. He also could not be charged with heterodoxy or heresy. In his pontificate, which began in 1878, Leo made the medieval Thomist synthesis the official approach to teaching in Catholicism. This made him a great champion of "natural law" and led him to see how many modern social arrangements violated such natural law.

Leo's encyclicals after 1885 began to define the spiritual and temporal powers (1885); speak up for the freedom of citizens (1888); and advocate Christian democracy (1891). *Rerum Novarum* in 1891 was his most sweeping and most invoked statement on the church in the modern world. When American social Christianity took shape, its advocates always appealed to him. This made them doctrinal conservatives but they were also social progressives.

Social Catholicism, to press further toward definition of what has to remain ill-defined, walked a narrow line. It would be voluntary and persuasive, yet in the end it had to work for legislation. Legislation in the secular order coerces. The policies would make room for the state and the public order to provide the framework for the justice Christians sought. They did not, however, want the state to have unlimited temporal powers and not any spiritual powers. They would promote new concepts of the stewardship of private possessions, yet Leo's tradition never went along with the socialists and communists in condemning private property. For these reasons the heritage of Leo XIII has been invoked by both sides within later Catholicism. The progressives welcomed its sense of corporate existence and its provision for governmental involvement in human welfare. The conservatives welcomed its insistence on private property and its unwillingness to yield individual stewardship to anything under state control.

American Catholic social thought and action were not, or at least not always, the products of people who spent their hours poring over papal encyclicals and the precedents of people like Bishop Ketteler. They were sometimes visionary, charismatic, and naive people who saw with horror what the modern industrial city was doing to make victims of Catholics and other people. These men began to keep company with non-Catholics who shared such a vision. In the most celebrated pioneering case, Father Edward McGlynn, who died in 1900, was devoted to the "Single Tax" theories of a progressive favorite, non-Catholic visionary Henry George. In 1886 McGlynn supported George's futile run for mayor of New York. This act stirred to a rage the blood of Archbishop Michael Corrigan. McGlynn would not be silent when Corrigan, a foe of George, tried to suppress the priest. In 1887 McGlynn was removed from his pastorate. McGlynn also refused a summons from Leo XIII, an act that was to end his potency as a Catholic. It also spread guilt by association among Catholic progressives who were faithful and obedient.

Catholicism, however, does allow for new beginnings. Through the agency of Archbishop Satolli, the papal delegate to the United States and later a firm antiprogressive, McGlynn began to work his way back. Satolli declared that the Georgean system did not violate Catholic teaching, even if it was not to be seen by any means as privileged within Catholicism. After some laundering by professors at the Catholic University, the wayward priest in 1893 was welcomed home. Rome made ever more consistent criticisms of the Single Tax approach but did not do so publicly. The Vatican even passed on word to Corrigan that it opposed the progressive theory, but did not want any condemnation published. It happens that down in Baltimore Cardinal Gibbons, again with a fine sense of timing and discretion, made clear to Rome that he feared a condemnation. This would only make George's theory and McGlynn's practice appear alluring at a time when both were on the wane. So McGlynn lived out the rest of his priesthood after 1893 in relative quiet. The mantle of social Catholic leadership was to pass to other more orthodox and practical leadership in the new century.

Progressivism   Bridging the centuries was the long-lived and tireless Monsignor John Augustine Ryan. His name is not well known to the public, including the Catholic public, today. One should be careful about resorting to "great hero" (or "great villain," in the eyes of some schools of Catholics) approaches in respect to a movement so broad as social Catholicism. At times the new public sense seems simply to have been "in the air," for any lay person, pastor, or bishop to grasp and employ. Yet if there was one individual who gave voice to this form of Christianity, it was Ryan. He merits notice.

Ryan, who lived from 1869 to 1945, was a Minnesotan who attended seminary in St. Paul in the 1890s. He then went on to a doctorate at Catholic University. A faculty member at the St. Paul school and later at his doctoral alma mater, Ryan taught until 1939. His career thus bridged two centuries. He also helped form a bridge between European precedent and American practice, between the teachings of Leo XIII and the United States leadership, between clergy and laity, religious and secular forces, the bishops and the government.

St. Paul was a center of progressivism. Archbishop John Ireland, an Americanizer, encouraged his seminarians to read the papal encyclical of 1891. It might be said that social Catholicism in America was born in the library and dormitory room of Ireland's seminary. Dutiful student John Ryan there worked to connect his own social impulses with the pope's teaching. There was nothing guileful at all about his use of Leo XIII on the American scene. Ryan enjoyed six decades of activity and expression. He could be tested a thousand ways and times. He believed the papal teaching because it was the voice of the pope and the church and was true. He supported it because it seemed intrinsically true in its address to natural law and needs for social justice and because it worked in the hands of pragmatists like Ryan and his allies in church and state. He would put this synthesis to work, always claiming, usually successfully, that his side was the pope's side. His achievement is best understood in that light.

The church with which Ryan and his colleagues worked prospered in its new status, no longer as a mission and in a nation filling with immigrants from Catholic Europe. In 1910 the Catholic Church claimed the loyalty of over 16,000,000 and through the next decade would approach 20,000,000 followers. This occurred mostly as the result of immigration, partly through growth because of large Catholic families, and in some measure because the Paulists, the Church Extension Society, and other agencies worked to commend the church to America and Americans to the church. By now an active Catholic press had been formed, not only in dioceses but also nationally. Previous mention on these pages of interactions at provincial and plenary councils and in gatherings of archbishops suggests a united, coherent, resolved United States Catholic Church.

Appearances deceive. Through the second decade of the century it became clear that Catholicism was not an interactive, united body at all. There were few opportunities for concerted action. Bishops did not know each other. Friends and enemies of the church had difficulty getting it in focus. Curiously, practical adjustments to World War I life did more than any ecumenical or Catholic impulses to promote convergences.

As the war came, German Catholics, like German Lutherans and German Reformed and even some German Jews, were on the spot. Germany had developed a high culture of which its heirs were proud. After 1871 and the rise of imperial Germany, that nation was coming to be admired for its military power. Germans in America lauded that; imperial America well understood guns. From colonial times Germans had been accused of being "thick" in their enclaves, of sticking together and not wanting to interact with the larger society. As war loomed in Europe, America had no pre-cut policy for alliances. Until at least 1914 it was safe to admire Germany. Then, from 1914 to 1917, it was legal and not always unsafe to advocate neutrality.

As Woodrow Wilson's policies moved the United States to ally with England and France and against Germany, Catholics and other Germans in America began to be subjects of suspicion. The declaration of war in 1917 ended all luxurious sense of safety for pro-Germans in America. German terms began to be replaced by English ones. No longer could a person go to kindergarten or eat sauerkraut. The noble Teuton was replaced by the atrocity-working Hun or Boche. Catholic and other parochial schools in some states were for a time prohibited from using German in the classroom. It happened that the German-American Catholics, like Germans through the decades and Catholics through the century, very quickly lined up in loyalty to their nation in war time. Such Catholics joined others in promoting the war effort. They encouraged enlistment in the military, selling Liberty Bonds. The rhetoric of defensiveness by this element of the Catholic Church had to be matched by hyperpatriot nationalist sounds by other Catholics not of German background. The war served to make a more united church visible.

Program The government could hardly suspect a church that in 1917-18 produced but four conscientious objectors among the laity and not a pacifist priest anywhere. It could not overlook the million Catholic troops, on which it relied in a military of five million. It also could not find a *The* Catholic Church with which to deal. There were many practical reasons to promote such dealing. How would one minister to troops through the chaplaincy and religiously based social services? How to organize relief in French and Belgian cities, or anywhere after the war would end? How would one find a central pattern in a church that had had nothing like a plenary council since 1884, a full third of a century before? Who knew whether the mobile and willing Knights of Columbus spoke for the church or was but one among many voluntary organizations?

In August of 1917 several hierarchs tried to meet this problem by helping convoke a meeting in Washington. Prominent in its affairs was a gifted and articulate Paulist, Father John J. Burke, of the *Catholic World* magazine. He knew his way around America, as a Paulist should, and around the church, as an editor should. He helped bring together a number of independent voluntary groups—agents of education, charity, chaplaincy, and the like.

As so often happens, the organizer gets or is left with the hard follow-up work. Burke was elected to head the resulting National Catholic War Council. Being practical and anticipating ecumenical times, Burke immediately reached out. The Federal Council of Churches was seeing a rise in morale and a growth in agenda as a uniting Protestant voice. He connected with its leadership, as well as with Jews. When the Secretary of War named "The Committee of Six" to represent religion, he turned to Burke. Burke's acceptability was a tribute to him and to the long set-apart and suspect Catholic Church.

Now, at last, Catholicism had found an instrument for carrying on common action. The council deferred to bishops, especially to Rockford, Illinois' Peter J. Muldoon, to assure that episcopal leadership would be attended to. Yet bishops had dioceses to which to return, while bureaucrats stayed on, in this case quite logically in Washington. There men like Burke could help establish policy. At the same time, lay expertise was called for in new ways. The NCWC became their instrument.

Armistice in November, 1918, meant that the NCWC should have outlived its usefulness and set out now to disband. Cynics would say that it was typical of a board or bureaucracy to know how to survive. Utopians would say that God had now provided the means through which the Catholic future could emerge. Practical-minded people between them say that Catholic leadership saw that peace, as well as war, called for common action. It is convenient to see the "W" for "War" in the NCWC name as a leftover seeking replacement. It came in the form of a substituted "W" for "Welfare." The council awaited a new agenda.

Enter Ryan. Back in 1906 he had published a short book on *A Living Wage*. He advocated a number of changes in the economy. Now Ryan was poised to present such arguments on the new national forum. Together with the administrative leadership of the NCWC he came forward in 1919 with *Social Reconstruction: A General Review of the Problems and Survey of the Remedies*. Ever since people have referred to it as the *Bishops' Program of Social Reconstruction*. It gave expression to Ryanism, which meant Leoism, applied in an industrial republic. This Ryanesque document was anything but the socialism its enemies saw in it. Yet it advocated governmental participation, not government neutrality or passivity, in the search for justice and welfare.

Many of the proposals seem commonplace in tone and scope. If government could take care of people in "W" for "War," why not regard their needs for "W" or "Welfare" in a hostile, competitive society? Agencies that cared for the military should survive, and should include the returning veteran in their sphere. The living wage demanded support, just as child labor must finally be restricted.

Those who wonder just where women might come in with respect to justice and welfare would be disappointed. Attacks on Ryan and the bishops for being particularly villainous as

Catholics, however, would be misplaced. They were not alone in seeing the causes of women only partially, with a general blind spot. It has been frequently shown that the Protestant social gospel also had no sight of or place for women. The Protestant leaders, perceived as radical in many respects, retained Victorian visions of the role of women. They equated these with the Bible's or the Christian traditions. Ryan also meant well in seeking welfare by keeping families strong and urging women to stay home to tend them. During the war many of them had replaced men in industrial jobs, or had taken new ones to advance military production. They should return now, from the dirty, demeaning work back to the sane and sanitary setting of the home. When they must and did work, Ryan and the committee statement urged, they should receive equal pay for equal work. In that one respect, at least, he was ahead of his time.

Woman suffrage, the Nineteenth Amendment, passed in June of 1919 and went into effect in August of 1920, without help from the Bishops' Program. Some charged that there was even foot-dragging and opposition on the part of the male leadership of the Catholic Church. Woman suffrage was coming to be typecast as an issue. Some claimed it tangled with birth control advocacy or was tainted, believe that or not, with the bolshevism that was abhorrent to Catholics and other Americans. Despite official frowns, however, Catholic lay women in key states like Massachusetts did rally and help lead the suffrage forces. When suffrage came, Ryan, who was moderate on the subject, paid respects to women. Maybe, he thought, they would bring some of their sanity to the voting booth, which needed it.

Bureaucrats who wrote the Bishops' Program feared bureaucracy and thus opposed socialism on that and other grounds. Yet they inaugurated a tradition that tempered the free enterprise capitalism by a call for drastic reforms. It focused on better working conditions, the living wage for laborers, and a critique of grossly disproportionate acquisitions of wealth by employers and owners. Monopolies were enemies and partnerships were allies in this program. As cautious as all this might have sounded fifty years later, it was bold in its own day. Naturally, it received a mixed reading among the bishops, including Gibbons, whose support was necessary despite his great age and waning power. Some bishops felt that not only did it not speak for them but even competed against them. For two or three years the NCWC stood a good chance of being terminated. Then, gradually, the faction of bishops who favored it prevailed. It was to serve constructive purposes through the New Deal era and beyond.

One way to write a summary of the NCWC is to suggest that in many respects its "secular" program matched the main outlines of New Deal legislation. Ryan promoted its activities throughout that period. His biography is named *Right Reverend New Dealer*. He supported the election of Franklin D. Roosevelt in 1933. Roosevelt appointed him to a board position a year later. Through the years Ryan published articles, pamphlets, and books advocating positions he first began to form while reading Leo's encyclicals in that library back in St. Paul. His steadfast Catholicism was most visible in his book of 1922, *The State and the Church*. Ryan rewrote it with Francis Boland in 1940 as *Catholic Principles of Politics*. Little Protestant children of my vintage were always able to be frightened by "Ryan and Boland," since the thesis was European-sounding enough to give rise to fears that an America that became 51 percent Catholic would be run by Catholics. The teaching on church and state became such a prominent feature that many non-Catholics overlooked Ryan's crusading for positions they otherwise favored. In any case, social Catholicism had, through the activities of Burke and Ryan and others, become a part of the formal life of the church. It was no longer voiced by the mavericks at the margins.

Complications

Anti-Catholic social activity and anti-social Catholicism lived on, complicating the life of the victorious and diminishing the scope of their victories. By anti-Catholic one can mean an array of forces from earlier populism to the Ku Klux Klan and immigration exclusion acts or to opposition to a Catholic presidential candidate in the twenties. Antisocial Catholicism appeared in the form of a social-sounding program in the thirties, under Father Charles Coughlin. Each deserves mention.

Populism and the Populist party should have been natural allies for rural Catholics and for many urban progressives. Yet it took rise in Midwestern and Southern states where there was some native anti-Catholicism. Under the leadership of people who often were anti-Catholic for personal reasons, it took a nasty turn. Thomas E. Watson, a Georgian who was the Populist candidate for president in 1904, carried his anti-Catholic mouthings all the way to the United States Senate. Under the encouragement of demagogues like Watson a new wave of anti-Catholic organizations formed in the teens of the century. Symbiotically, Catholic self-defense organizations countered, and the two worked out their unlovely charades at the edges of American respectability.

As Populist credibility declined and the self-defenders boasted that they had successfully put it down, an uglier form of anti-ism rose in the 1920s. The Ku Klux Klan, an anti-Negro organization in the South after the Civil War, was reorganized and took on new life. This time it was more ecumenical, since its old-stock WASP members, the displaced and resentful of the earth, included as scapegoats and enemies Jews and Catholics along with blacks. The Klan moved north. Whoever has seen a cross burn, visualized a lynching, or known the effects of the Klan on legislators, has reasons to feel a chill at the mention of the word. To see the Klan become strong and almost respectable in a northern state like Indiana well into the twentieth century is to inspire fear, almost panic. Yet, as so often before and sometimes since, the Klan served mainly to remind people of how many bizarre creatures crawl around under the planks of a diverse society. As years passed, its threat also largely passed. Fears of Catholicism were then transferred to more potent mainstream channels.

Sometimes the new legislation was obviously intrusive. In Alabama there were laws mandating convent inspection. More threatening was a case symbolized in law by *Pierce v. Society of the Sisters*. Oregon had passed a law in its effort to close parochial schools and force all children into public schools. In 1925 the United States Supreme Court struck that down as unconstitutional. Equally threatening and with more permanent effects was anti-immigration legislation of the mid-decade. It was designed to limit the arrivals of Orientals, Hispanics, and any number of other newcomers in the interest of preserving old-stock America. Yet inevitably it focused on European Catholics of the wrong sort. The Reed-Johnson Act of 1924 introduced a quota system based on the numbers of immigrants that had been permitted from each nation decades before, back when approved peoples dominated among the newcomers. Three-fourths of the unacceptables, it turned out, came from eastern and southern Europe a decade before the law. It was their flow that the legislators thought had to be stopped. It was. Mexicans, however, made up for excluded Europeans, though in the 1930s attempts were made to begin to exclude them, too.

The presidential candidacy of Alfred E. Smith, Democratic governor of New York in 1928, provided still another opportunity for a focused anti-Catholicism. Smith was a "wet" who favored repeal of Prohibition, which was largely a Protestant cause. Most Protestants were "dry." Smith was a Democrat. In the age of "normalcy," of Harding and Coolidge and Hoover, the bulk of Protestant laity tended to vote Republican. The Catholic was boisterous and unrespectable and they were square and respectable. For these and a host of other reasons it has always been difficult for historians to sort out where and when anti-Catholicism played a part in his defeat. Doctoral candidates in political science can always whet their tools by publishing one more precinct-by-precinct analysis. They take sides in the question as to whether it was anti-Catholicism or anti-Smith-wet-Democratism that was responsible. As is often the case, the safest thing to say is also the most substantiable: voters are complex and campaigns more so. We can never sort out all the motives and interests. What can be said with assurance is that both overt and covert anti-Catholic expression did temporarily increase in 1928.

The Smith candidacy was troubling to Democratic progressives who did not like his style or his connections with political bossism yet who found the Herbert Hoover campaign a problem in respect to social causes. Protestant theologians, intellectuals, and editors found it necessary and respectable to voice fears of Catholic power while opposing Smith. Issues as old as those that afflicted Bishop John Carroll a century and a half earlier were resurrected. Could the church of the *Syllabus of Errors* and papal infallibility really now permit a United States chief executive to act on the basis of his oath and his conscience? The most frequently told story of the tension and the way Smith sought to minimize it, possibly apocryphal or at least dressed up, bears retelling. A Protestant lawyer named Charles G. Marshall pretentiously wrote "An Open Letter to the Honorable Alfred E. Smith." The key question: how would Smith as president handle his office if he had to cope with an encyclical that compromised his American commitment? The purported answer of Smith: "Will somebody please tell me what in hell an encyclical is?" The story gains when it is oral, complete with the pronunciation "enkyklical." We *do* know that Smith called in counselors to help draft a response that should have satisfied all, but did not.

Can anything be said for the Marshalls, the editors of *The Christian Century*, the denominational periodicals and church-state experts in Protestantism who expressed some fears? Yes, if one keeps in mind the context of the period. Their reaction was inexplicable to longtime American Catholics, who had never shown a trace of disloyalty to America. It was explicable to non-Catholics who knew the European tradition, read Ryan on church and state, and expected consistency. The *Syllabus of Errors* and the modern papal tradition did threaten complications. The growth of Catholicism did seem to bode ill for the democratic process. The problem was that those fears could induce paranoia and panic and promote ill will between Catholic and non-Catholic neighbors. After the Smith campaign, it should be said, popular anti-Catholicism evidently diminished through the next decade as Americans united behind new issues during the Great Depression.

What we are calling, with a tinge of irony, antisocial Catholicism appeared as a popular movement in the 1930s as a result of response to the Great Depression. The irony comes in because its progenitor, Father Charles Coughlin, advocated policies that had social and solidaristic intent—but of a sort that eventually were perceived as rightwing, or, more crudely and crassly, as Fascist in tendency.

Father Coughlin was not the most representative American Catholic of the 1930s, but he was certainly by far the best known. The Ontario-born priest in 1926 was assigned to a pastorate in Royal Oak, Michigan. A genius at promotion and self-promotion, Coughlin named it the Shrine of the Little Flower, to capitalize on the then current interest in Saint Thérèse of Lisieux, "the Little Flower," who was attracting a working-class following.

Coughlin missed no opportunity to build up his parish. He cajoled celebrities, especially baseball players—he had been a good one himself—into appearing at his church for fundraisers. When the Ku Klux Klan marched in Royal Oak, Coughlin parodied and defused it by marching along. But when the Klan then reverted to style and burned a cross at the Shrine's yard, Coughlin was given time on Detroit's WJR to defend Catholicism.

Radio and Coughlin were made for each other. Fifteen minutes spent with old recordings of his voice show why. The priest could play to emotions, move crowds, and inspire confidence and action. It was said that as his own broadcast grew, which meant after he introduced social programs to give hope to Detroit's and America's Depression victims, the audience grew to several millions—by no means all of them Catholic. Could there have been forty million listeners each Sunday? Scientific measuring devices were then undeveloped. Researchers make guesses based on mail response and knowledge that many kinds of local activities had to be postponed everywhere when Father Coughlin "came on."

It took some time for Coughlin to find policies to go with his voice and his promise. At first the Detroit archbishop favored this eloquent apologist. Monsignor John A. Ryan thought him an ally. Franklin D. Roosevelt briefly welcomed his support.

Martin E. Marty

Some Jews saw Coughlin's critiques of capitalism to be congenial. Then, at first subtly and soon drastically, he broke old ties and moved in new directions as he thought about what he believed and would support. He turned vehemently on Roosevelt, who was glad for a public breach when Coughlin became an embarrassment. The archbishop of Detroit eventually had no choice but to oppose him. Jews fled for cover.

The heart of Coughlinism was expressed in his National Union for Social Justice after 1934 and his journal, *Social Justice*, after 1936. The priest would do away with private banking and thus eliminate the international cabal of cunning Jewish bankers. He would dissolve unions and nationalize some processes and resources. The government would take control of banking policies. It would also turn its back on allies who were ready to fight the Nazi and Fascist threats in Europe.

Coughlin made a great mistake when in 1936 he tested his voting strength. Having a large radio audience of sympathizers was one thing. Having people stake their futures on him when Roosevelt and Republican Alfred M. Landon were the live options was another. His Union Party candidate William Lemke was defeated so grandly that Coughlin should have been disgraced. Yet he left the air only briefly, thus keeping a promise associated with such a defeat, only to return a few weeks later with a bolder program, voiced more nastily. He became overtly anti-Semitic and in some respects pro-Nazi. Coughlin opposed America's entry into the war on the side it did, for the causes it did. The archbishop forced him off the air, and Coughlin had enough respect for Catholic authority to obey. His magazine was suppressed by governmental mail policies.

From 1942 to his death in 1966 Coughlin lived on with his parishioners, his scrapbooks and memories, his relative silence— only to lift his voice now and then to show that he could be

162

secluded but not convinced. He opposed Communism or anything that looked like it, including the Second Vatican Council, which was too ambiguous for him. Were it not for his millions of hearers, readers, and partisans, he would be easy to dismiss as an eccentric, as mere evidence that America has room for every kind. Because of them, however, latter-day Catholics and other citizens have to ponder the base of his support and appeal in the discontents induced by the Depression. That he could invoke, or believe that he was invoking, papal social teachings only demonstrates how confusing were the times, how ambiguous were some of the possible applications of that tradition.

It would be unfair to leave the thirties with only the taste of Coughlin in the mouth. One could point to many kinds of vitalities, not only on the side of Ryan but also among Catholic conservatives who kept opposing the New Deal. There were also energies devoted by the journal, *The Commonweal,* to giving a voice to Catholic laity, as Catholics had to make sense of the Spanish Civil War, the rise of Nazism, and the later stages of New Deal life before World War II.

Historians who point to these vitalities find it valid and necessary to focus on individual cities. No matter how sweeping the programs of the NCWC, creative footdragging by local bishops could retard everything, while impulse by others would advance such programs. In most reckonings, the archdiocese of Chicago is singled out as exemplary. Its archbishop George William Mundelein is often seen as the paradigm of the personal policy of Corporation Sole, as the title of his biography would have it. He administered and "owned" the property of this largest diocese in the nation. Named to the Chicago post in 1915, he became a doer on the grand scale. His St. Mary of the Lake Seminary at, naturally, Mundelein, near Chicago, was to have been a university. It was and is an architectural example of Catholic American triumphalism. The chapel is American colonial in style, done up with Catholic ornateness. There is a Barberini ceiling in the library to recall a favorite site from Mundelein's years of study in Rome. His own residence on the grounds across the little lake is Mount Vernonesque, but marbled more than wooden. Mundelein attracted notice by hosting the Eucharistic Congress in Chicago in 1926. He flexed Catholic muscle in the metropolis that was so stocked with immigrant groups that it looked like "Little Europe." It was also, through his ministrations, hyper-America.

Mundelein lived until 1939, the year the war broke out. Fear or deride him as one may, he also provoked and inspired respect for the ways in which he fought off antisocial Catholicism. This approach led him to early condemnations of Nazism and Fascism and support for preparedness. But by 1939 all that had not yet become his church's major agenda item. There were first the needs of urban-industrial Catholics and other citizens for which to care. Mundelein then drew on the social progressive tradition and encouraged or allowed the growth of many movements.

It was under his tutelage, for example, that the Catholic Youth Organization under the colorful Auxiliary Bernard Sheil prospered. Sheil stayed on the front pages for a couple of decades, usually on the side of the workers, if not the angels. He was a fundraiser, organizer, inspirer of the young, nudger of politicians, despair of the conservative press. He found company in Father Reynold Hillenbrand, a pioneer in liturgical reform in America. Liturgical reform later was often seen as an activity of specialists, of scholarly and esthetic temperaments, of people who seemed far from the social action scene. Hillenbrand and his seminarians were not. They conceived liturgy as "the people's service." They wanted to link up with the people who suffered the hurts of the Depression, the anxieties of joblessness, the hopes for better times. Mundelein's successor, Cardinal Samuel Stritch, followed these policies for two more decades. Out of Chicago came the Catholic—later the Christian—Family Movement, a Catholic Interracial Council, and many admired and later controversial examples of a lay apostolate. Other dioceses had more conservative and even repressive leadership, but in them as well as at other progressive centers, a new lay apostolate, with clerical support, was taking shape. This all added variety to American Catholicism in a time when the Coughlins would cast it on Fascist lines and when non-Catholics miscast it as simply subservient to a grasping, repressive Rome.

Achievement

Achievement marked the life of the church as it approached midcentury. The Depression economy and mood yielded to the sense of sacrifice and purpose that came with World War II. This was the "last good war," good because for the last time the vast majority of the American people were able to unite in interpreting and supporting it. The threat to civilization represented by the Axis was so obvious and the demand for a common response to that threat was so vivid that citizens fell in line, with Catholics often ahead in the ranks. This time there were a few more Catholic conscientious objectors to military service; the four of World War I were succeeded by several hundred in World War II. Most of these were followers of Peter Maurin and Dorothy Day; they were pacifists who had ties to the Catholic Worker Movement. While these objectors were individually stigmatized, they created no scandal of the Catholic Church itself.

165

Instead, the church supplied men and women for service, offered support for their efforts, and provided chaplains for their spiritual care. In one famous instance, a Catholic chaplain was seen to have been going down with his ship. The priest was praying in company with Protestant and Jewish counterparts. The group became a feature of World War II iconography and cherished memory.

As is often the case, the church offered more by way of morale support than might have been necessary. One reads the hyperbole about American righteousness in contrast to the demonic—and it was demonic—character of the enemy and wonders where the prophetic note then went. Dorothy Dohen serves us by reproducing samples from Cardinal Francis Spellman, who merits notice here. Spellman, the son of a Massachusetts grocer and his wife, was the best known hierarch after Cardinal Gibbons, who flourished one war earlier. Spellman is a case study in "making it" by playing the rules of the game. Not remembered today for pastoral depth or spiritual profundity, he knew how to use political power and mass media of communications.

Spellman made use of connections he had made in Rome in the 1920s to advance himself in the 1930s. One break came for him when he connected visiting Cardinal Eugenio Pacelli with Franklin Delano Roosevelt. In 1939 Pacelli became pope. He appointed Spellman to the New York archiepiscopate and to be the United States Air Forces military vicar. He would use both bases to influence the next four presidents and to interpret Catholicism to America and America to Catholicism. His was a language of almost complete identification between divine and American purposes, of almost complete disregard for the notion that the Lord of the heavens laughed at the pretensions of all nations. Such rhetorical flourishes served him and the

Catholicism of his day well. Both were high achievers. Both had a need to bask as they summoned energies for new purposes.

Dohen literally overheard Spellman say that the "white" of the flag stood for "the basic righteousness of our national purpose." One of his prayer poems ends: "We are a single host of grateful love for Thee, A single will for universal peace of men, A single soul of righteousness to come!" In all of this there remained no hint of Catholic isolation or distance from cultural bondage. Spellman provided theory for his venture: "Leaders of a religion will espouse nationalism, not simply to keep their church acceptable in a pluralist society, but out of the same need for identity and the sense of belonging that motivates all people in the given society." The cardinal lived out his theory.

When World War II came, Spellman had his chance to fuse American and Catholic purposes. "Our President and our Holy Father have combined the forces of our great country, and the forces of religion in a battle for peace. . . ." He compared the death of American service people with the crucifixion of Christ. "Then a Man suffered and died to save his fellow man . . . . These young American airmen with whom I was living wanted to believe and did believe that they too were suffering and dying to bring salvation and peace to their fellow men. . . ." The archbishop has *The Risen Soldier* saying, in Spellman-style poetry: "And if it be/ My blood should mingle reverently with Christ's, his son's, in this my final missioning,/ Shall I not whisper with my dying breath—'Lord, it is sweet to die . . . for these United States,/ Which, in your wisdom, you have willed should be/ A beacon to the world'. . . ."

The war ended and Spellman, his diocese—which he administered magisterially—and his church prospered. As the Cold War replaced World War II, the church for the most part joined in the spirit of a "crusade against atheistic Communism." At the

167

end of the Truman era and the beginning of the Eisenhower era, during and after the Korean War for which Spellman again tried to provide morale and ideology, some other Americans and some American Catholics turned legitimate fear of communism overseas and subversion at home into a version of the crusade that showed signs of paranoia. These were the years when Senator Joseph McCarthy of Wisconsin gained fame for his activities and efforts to find and ferret out communists from civilian and military service. McCarthy was a Catholic who was favored by many right-wing fellow believers. Anti-McCarthyites looked to the church for repudiations of the senator and his tactics. Some interfaith strains appeared when few condemnations were forthcoming. Dissenting Catholic minorities also attacked him, but he remained a favorite of many highly placed leaders. Our Lady of Fatima had prophesied conflict with Russia. Catholics were forming prayer circles and establishing novenas to help carry out divine purposes against the center of the communist empire. McCarthy seemed to provide documentation for the holy cause.

Prosperity McCarthy, in the end, was to self-destruct. While the church remained alert against communism, it also had other things on its mind. The sense of achievement now was able to be put to work for new gains. Several years after the war it was clear that some sort of religious revival was going on. Military people, back from their uprooting, settled with large families on campuses and then in suburbs. The G.I. Bill made college education a practical reality for millions of young people from Catholic homes in which they were the first family members ever to attend college. In the suburbs they broke up the old ethnic ghettos of the cities.

Where their ethnic backgrounds had once provided identity, now the church did.

Will Herberg in 1955 offered a popular explanation, one that goes a long way though not far enough to explain the revival and its shape. In *Protestant-Catholic-Jew* Herberg noticed that the old "melting pot" described at the turn of the century had not melted all peoples and paths into a single mold. It was true that there *was* a single mold, a kind of religious support for "the American Way of Life," which Dwight Eisenhower promoted benignly and Spellman touted with biblical and Catholic identifications. Yet there were several ways to do this promoting. Few Americans supported this American Way directly. Most did it through three great conglomerates, marked in the title by names for three faiths. Herberg's three, it was soon seen, were far too few. But he did notice an application of an observation about immigration: what the son wants to forget the grandson wants to remember. The Polish or Italian Catholic immigrant child could and would have to leave behind the Old Country language and customs. The grandchild would try to do some retrieving. It was possible to recapture names and menus and the decor of life. For substance, the most recoverable element was the religion of grandparents.

Insofar as this explanation explained, it showed how and why religions converged in that time and spirit of consensus. Enormous tensions and conflicts did remain. Harry S. Truman in 1950-51 wanted to turn the representation of Myron C. Taylor at the Vatican into ambassadorial recognition. A Holy War of words immediately erupted between Catholics and non-Catholics. Protestants fought Catholics over public support of school buses for parochial school children. Paul Blanchard made an industry of attacking Catholic power. A militant watchdog group on "the wall of separation between church and state," named "Protestants and Other Americans United for Separation of Church and State," intended to be generally vigilant, but instead focused chiefly on Catholicism. Liberals like the editors of *The Christian Century* looked on at Catholic growth as much as did Fundamentalists: "Can Catholicism Win America?" asked a series and a book by the *Century* editor in 1951. His answer, and that of many other worriers, was "Yes, it could," to the detriment of the Republic. Nostalgia for the Eisenhower era of good feeling from the retrospect of later times of raw conflict glosses over such tensions and flaps. Whoever would forget need only revisit the record of a contretemps between Spellman and Eleanor Roosevelt, a classic case of misreading and overstating by both sides.

Having said all that, one must still say that the fifties were good times not only for religion in general but for Catholicism in particular. During the 1950s the Catholic population, thanks to a baby boom and the religious renewal, grew by an incredible 44 percent, while the number of children in parochial schools grew by 66 percent. In 1950 there were 43,000 priests and in 1960 there were 54,000, while seminarians who had only 388 seminaries from which to choose in 1950 had 525 in 1960. The number preparing for priesthood moved from 26,000 to about 40,000. The church had never known such a moment.

Catholicism was part of the billion-dollar-a-year building boom in religion, back when a billion dollars was more than loose change and still bought something. An achieving people built with marble and walnut in the new churches, convents, and seminaries. A Shrine of the Immaculate Conception in Washington, D.C. symbolized Catholic arrival and power.

More than ever before, Catholicism provided figures who were recognized far beyond the sphere of one church. Bishop Fulton Sheen in the fifties used his European training in

Thomism and his personal charisma to become the first religious television celebrity. Millions of Catholics were informed by his weekly programs, and non-Catholics were also attracted. Thus Thomas Merton, a rakehell with literary gifts, in 1941 turned to the Trappists. He led a generation of post-war seekers to the monastic life. Through the decade Merton provided some of the more serious spiritual fare in books on the contemplative life. For the first time monasticism of the strictest sort became comprehensible to non-Catholics, thanks to his eloquence and example. The Abbey of Gethsemani became a pilgrimage goal so attractive that it was hard for the Cistercians there to keep the quiet needed for their style of devotion. New monasteries rose and old ones prospered. *The Seven Storey Mountain* of Merton's autobiography attracted other climbers. *The Waters of Siloe* and *Seeds of Contemplation* about which Merton wrote lured many to spiritual reflection in what W. H. Auden was calling *The Age of Anxiety,* a time of restlessness amid relative prosperity.

Dorothy Day, a remarkable convert whom some have mentioned as a candidate for sainthood, was known for far more than having inspired some pacifists in World War II. After a young adulthood of drift and rebellion, she joined the church, left behind a common-law husband and carried responsibility for a daughter ahead. Instead of spending her time at the farm where colleague Peter Maurin operated a sort of commune, she promoted "solidaristic" (her enemies said "socialistic") styles of Catholicism. Her opponents in California addressed her in other terms. She first was visible in the cause on May Day, 1933. She and colleagues then began peddling a one-cent *Catholic Worker* in New York's Union Square. The "harsh and dreadful love" of which Dostoevsky had spoken, became so much a part of her search for justice that a biographer later used the phrase in a book title about Day. The Catholic Worker movement sponsored homes for the poor. Day's fine-featured and intense face took on almost iconic significance. A stern, self-disciplined, again, "charismatic" person, Day was never fashionably "in" and never unfashionably "out." She stuck to her vision, which combined a relatively conservative convert-Catholicism with a radical social outlook. She did so with a compelling integrity that led many Catholics and others to examine conscience and probe their own styles.

Intellectuality In 1955 the premier Catholic historian John Tracy Ellis looked back on the intellectual efforts of ghetto existence, as he and others called it. Catholics had retreated into their ethnic and parochial enclaves for a century and had had little impact on the national intellectual ethos. Most Catholic universities were mediocre, and they were not upgrading enough during the decade of prosperity in the 1950s. Lay people did not put sufficient premium on the life of the mind. Where were the Catholic scientists?

Ellis was a sympathetic critic, sometimes understandably still defensive in his championing of the beleaguered church into the 1950s. As an historian, Ellis was aware of causes behind the ghetto mentality. He knew about Vatican discouragements of theological exploration ever since the condemnations of modernism in 1907-08. He discerned why wary Catholic educators remained timid and cautious. Ellis knew that they were more interested in passing on old knowledge than seeking the new. Theology was in an ossified state. The church expected theologians to be antique shopkeepers of the faith, the museum guardians. He also knew that the church was in a world that gave the Christian faith little quarter and would not listen simply because the numbers of those attending Mass was growing.

This did not mean that there were no celebrators of mind or contributors to learning. After some decades we can look back and remember people like the Columbia University historian of nationalism, Carleton J.H. Hayes. Yves Simon and Jacques Maritain came to America to champion neo-Thomism. They made their mark on the academy. Political scientists like Jerome Kerwin were unself-conscious about their church and faith on secular campuses. Priests and nuns studied on such campuses with more frequency than ever before. Individuals among them were writing publishable doctoral theses that were of wide influence. Yet there were particular inhibitions against theological experiment.

Even that was beginning to change. Father Gustave Weigel, S.J., was a leader at the Jesuit powerhouse named Woodstock in Maryland. He became the first well-known agent for the ecumenical cause. In a book with Protestant Robert McAfee Brown, Weigel spelled out rules for dialogue that soon became useful as Catholics were allowed, even urged, to pursue such conversations. Weigel tirelessly made the circuit of campuses, conferences, and radio interview shows to display very sophisticated modern understandings of faith that were in every sense in the classic traditions of open orthodoxy.

To describe the climate of that era and the daring of people like Weigel is difficult to a generation or two that cannot remember, and was not even alive or adult, before the Second Vatican Council. Personal recall might illustrate the point. While Catholics in the fifties partook in discussions of pluralism at the juncture of religious-and-secular, Christian-and-Jewish spheres, they were very cautious about Christian ecumenical encounters. They could be alluring, compromising; they could lead to "indifferentism." Such meetings were especially watched. Yet the Benedictines at St. John's University and the Holy Cross Fathers under Father Theodore Hesburgh at Notre Dame began to invite Protestant and Orthodox theologians to their campuses to discuss the faith. This they did, at first tentatively, and then with surprising ease. Yet there was caution about the spiritual dimension. At both places, on the eve of the Council, the hosts were granted permission for the sessions to conclude with a lit candle and the Lord's Prayer—but participants were not to tell the press or others about this pioneering kind of prayerful activity. That the church later changed was a tribute not only to Pope John XXIII and his kind, if he has a kind. It was also the result of activities by people like Fathers Weigel and Hesburgh, who played by the rules of the games and stayed mentally in the roomy mansions of orthodoxy—and then pushed as far as they could under the circumstances.

One turns the page on this era aware that too little has been said about new vitalities. Lay initiative was a key to changes. *The Commonweal* and *The Critic* opened literary worlds for the Catholic reader. The Christian Family Movement taught loyalty to family and church and then called Catholics to the public sphere. Many people, known and unknown, made their contributions within the confines of a church just moving out of the ghetto, monitored by Rome, still partly suspect in society. They were on the verge of something new. It is hard, however, to find references by any social scientist, theologian, or other person of responsibility, who foresaw the Catholic encounters with the modern world that resulted from the activities of three men named John: John F. Kennedy, John Courtney Murray, and Pope John XXIII. At the turn between the fifties and the sixties they and what they led or symbolized led to a turn between ages. No one knew better than they that they were building upon the achievement of millions through the mid-century decades. Achievements when these were gross came to be called "triumphalism"; when confined they were still of the "ghetto." There were other ways which brought their own problems and possibilities—awaiting a church and society that did not expect their arrival in the 1960s. The Spirit, like the wind, blows when and where it will.

CHAPTER SIX

The Pluralists:
1960-1985

Pluralism   Pluralism can mean, and to the philoso-
phers does mean, that the truth at the
heart and limit of the universe, which
means "metaphysically," is plural, many-fold. Most citizens,
however, have more modest uses in mind. In slang language, the
word stands for a polity in which "any number can play," and
many groups, especially religious groups, do. It is a term that
intends to describe a society in which people who occupy very
different universes of discourse and outlooks on life must coexist
and who want to do so with positive outcomes.

America was pluralist when Native American tribes developed
and displayed different languages, rites, and religious visions.
It was more vividly so when Catholics and then Protestants,
from Spain and France and then northern Europe set foot in the
New World. By the twentieth century a couple of hundred
denominations and religious interest groups and movements
complicated the lives of theological monists and democratic

simplists who wanted everyone to be like everyone else. How to live with pluralism was and was seen to be a special problem for Catholics. Officially their church taught that error did not have rights, and that non-Catholics were errorists. These had to be endured because they existed and would not go away. They might even be in the majority. Still, just as pluralism was messy for Protestants who would solve everything by a common return to the New Testament primitive church, so it was unsightly and chaotic to Catholics. They would resolve pluralism when all would acknowledge Christianity through obedience to the pope.

Through the 1950s Father John Courtney Murray began to ask Catholics and other Americans to come to terms with Catholicism and pluralism. The New York lawyer's son, a Jesuit who also taught at Woodstock, was particularly good at smoking out ideology in the political outlooks of Protestants and other Americans who thought they did not have one. They thought that only Catholics did. Murray could show, for example, how a Deist or Baptist view of the First Amendment had become privileged, one might say established, in a society that professed no establishment. He was a firm and orthodox defender of Catholicism. Fifteen years after his death he was looked back on as a conservative.

That reputation is ironic, given the pressures put upon Murray through the 1950s by conservative rivals in the priesthood. After a stint at Yale in 1951-52 he returned to Woodstock and editing roles for *Theological Studies*. There he presented his findings and theses about Catholicism and pluralism. These were disturbing to an Old Guard that had the ear of the Vatican and that succeeded in having him suppressed from time to time. He grew dispirited, almost despairing about making his point and at the same time remaining the obedient Jesuit that he was and that he wanted to be. Yet advocates kept making space for him, and the new spirit did not die. Murray returned repeatedly to Catholic and pluralist platforms and journals to make his careful case.

In Murray's view, religious pluralism was against the will of God, but it was the human condition. It would not marvelously cease to trouble the human city. Americans of competing interest groups should look for the minimal minimum of *consensus juris,* the agreement one needs to move beyond confusion to disagreement and thus to creative argument. On that basis they could converse and sometimes adjudicate differences, since one could have only confusion unless there were some common terms. Murray made much of "the American proposition" set forth in the Declaration of Independence and other founding documents.

A corollary of the changed conceptions Murray sought among American pluralists who wanted monopolies was a letting go of the impulse for monopoly in Catholicism. So his other voice was directed not at the public but at his own church. There he argued for the notion that error does have rights, that religious freedom was a basic right. Catholicism must recognize also that with which it does not agree. When the issue of religious freedom came up at the third session of Vatican Council II in 1964, Murray was the main advocate and drafter. When Vatican conservatives saw to the postponement of the issue and would work to defeat it, Murray was again dispirited, near despair. Yet with the strong efforts of bishops like Chicago's Cardinal Albert Meyer there was rallying of support between sessions. The Declaration of Religious Freedom was passed at the final session of the Council in 1965. A personal victory for Murray, a churchly and national victory for American Catholicism, it would have a bearing on Catholicism's situation everywhere in the world. The document represented one of many decisive changes at the Council. It remains a monument to Murray.

Politics

Murray had more successfully theorized about Catholicism in America than anyone in his church since at least Bishop John Carroll. He was a *Time*-cover scale celebrity. Yet his work was too cerebral and abstract to make him truly available to the public. The realization of what Catholic approaches to pluralism were about was better lived than advocated. The most visible symbol of its presence was President John F. Kennedy.

The story of the rise to office of this heir to two aggressive Boston Irish families need not be detailed here, because it belongs chiefly to political history. The reason for passing it up cannot any longer be because it is part of the personal memory of the majority of Catholics and other Americans. After more than a quarter century, more citizens than not had no living memory of the presidential campaign of Kennedy. Let it be only recalled that in 1928 his Catholicism was held against candidate Alfred E. Smith. Now some would also use his faith against the Massachusetts senator late into the 1950s, after the Catholic achievement had become so visible, while understandings of pluralism were growing.

Religion was an issue in a number of primaries, though Kennedy's chief competitor, Hubert H. Humphrey, who was on good terms with Catholic constituencies, was extremely careful not to make it an overt issue. The vigilant anti-Catholic, church/state and Protestant interest groups were chiefly responsible for exploiting uneasinesses in the general populace. In one pathetic, one might almost say desperate, attempt at coalition building, some fundamentalist-minded and some modernist-lineage Protestants, who could have agreed on nothing else, met to discuss the Catholic issue. Popular preacher Norman Vincent Peale, the best known attender, unfortunately for him found the press calling this "the Peale group." He backed away. In a highly publicized meeting with Protestant clergy at Houston, Kennedy dispelled fears. Catholicism began to become a nonissue in the election. At last pluralism was realized when a non-Protestant was chief executive.

Lay Catholic Kennedy, Harvard-schooled and not profoundly rooted in Catholic sources and ethos, became president of all the people. He reached out symbolically to the new generation. His 1000 days in office before his assassination found him with little formal accomplishment and with some embarrassments, like the Cuban Bay of Pigs disaster. Later revelations about his personal and political life stained his image.

There is no doubt, however, that Kennedy did much to change the climate of American life. Sociologist Robert N. Bellah in a famed essay of 1967 on America's civil religion saw Kennedy among the prime delineators of that generalizing tradition. At the very least, Kennedy showed an ease at handling his faith and his politics. He embodied the kind of pluralism for which Murray contended.

America could never again go back behind Kennedy to comprehend the worldview of fearful and defensive Protestant, anti-papal America. Tensions and conflicts would remain, as they will and must in the politics of a republic. Six campaigns later, in 1984, there were fresh debates about Catholic interventions in presidential politics. Some bishops then implied endorsements of one candidate because of his antiabortion stand. Now, however, the obvious divisions within the Catholic political community and the equally obvious divisions outside it, in respect to legal abortion or other issues, showed that pluralism was healthy. It followed new ground rules and had new outlines. Murray and the Catholic pluralists had never asked for simple concord—only for enough consensus to keep the argument going.

Aggiornamento The Catholic Church did not exist just for national life. As Pope John Paul II was to say back when he was archbishop of Cracow, "The church possesses a special interiority and a specific openness." The specific openness is directed to public life, where it in effect "calls its shots." The church keeps its integrity while pouring itself out for the surrounding world. Its "special interiority" calls for attention to its own inner life, dynamic, and agenda.

Ecumenism more than pluralism characterized that agenda in the new era. The prime character for the move into the era of realized ecumenism was no American at all. In fact he was someone who held little promise for Americans when he was elected in 1958. This third of the three men named John was Angelo Roncalli, who took the name John XXIII. He was clearly elected as a compromise or transition figure by warring parties in the cardinalate who wanted a time-bider. The Synod of Rome under his leadership promised little. Its concerns seemed to be focused on less than cosmic issues like whether nuns dared be seen on motor scooters. It is hard to find anyone who foresaw the Second Vatican Council, which John announced in 1961. It is almost as hard to locate any prophets who expected much of an ecumenical character when it convened for its first session in Rome after the autumn of 1962. At first glance the Council seemed to be devoted to housekeeping and minor housecleaning within the church. The bishops might have spent the time defining their role in the modern world. The first session had little to point to by way of achievement.

While Paul VI succeeded John XXIII after the first session, and while Paul should receive more credit than he usually gets for subsequent ecumenical achievement, it was John who had thrown open the doors. He spoke of *aggiornamento,* a creative shaking up of the church. Yet it was he who taught the church to regard Orthodox and Protestant Christians as "separated brothers" and sisters. Here one must resist temptations to retell the story of Popes John and Paul, to chronicle the Council, to follow all its declarations. With restraint, we turn its mirror back to America, the present subject.

The Council effected changes that only those who had come to maturity as faithful "pre-Vatican II" Catholics can appreciate in their brains and bones. After more than a generation a genre of literature and drama survived in which authors and audiences could revisit the Bad Old Days. These, however, had to be directed to the Senior Citizen generation. Writers first had to create a world that in some ways was as remote spiritually as the Middle Ages. Of course, there were continuities. The church's is mainly a story of continuities. The Mass remains the center of Catholic life. Priests take vows of celibacy and women are not ordained to the priesthood. Catholics baptize and believe in the grace of God. They pray and hope for eternal life with God. Yet discontinuities make up the drama of history, and the Catholic story in America after the three men named John has also been one of remarkable discontinuities.

So sudden were these changes, and so exuberantly were they exploited by a few extremists, that a cult of Catholic nostalgia quickly rose to counter them. Nostalgia, the rust of memory and not its steel, gives us the forties via the Andrews Sisters without World War II, the fifties through Elvis Presley and Norman Rockwell without Senator McCarthy and the Cold War. Catholic nostalgia gives us the Latin Mass as an esthetic construct without the numbing boredom that accompanied it for many. It provides the image of obedient sisters being passive and faithful without recalling the boredom, the repression, the meaningless penances, the depersonalization that could go with their convent way of life. It gives us theology untroubled by controversial visitors like Hans Küng or Edward Schillebeeckx without reminding us of the general lack of creativity, the unwillingness to dare as Augustine and Aquinas had dared to confront the worldviews of their day. It gives us Catholic bloc power and coercion without showing how devoid of democratic principle and unconcerned with rights such power-wielding could be.

The literature about the Good Old Days sees the American translation of Vatican II policies as the Bad New Days. Unquestionably the James Hitchcocks and George A. Kellys who write in such modes have plenty of documentation and can produce some legitimate tales of woe. Sometimes immediately after the Council liberty did turn to license. Some ex-priests told more about themselves than about their "outdated" church as they took their Oedipal tantrums about Il Papa in Rome and their rage about Mother Church in America into TV camera range.

The bill of particulars is lengthy. The Catholic reform came at a time of great societal unrest. The two fed each other and lived off each other. The Civil Rights movement and, for a time and in many ways, the Vietnam War protest cause called forth the best in the Catholic conscience. Catholics demonstrated the way of Christ and the place of the church when they responsibly argued and spoke up. Yet it was also clear that some were part of utopian movements that were not rooted in Catholicism nor congruent with its patterns. They used the symbolism of priesthood, sisterness, or lay Catholicism to advance their own shorter-term political causes. They looked merely embarrassing a few years later.

Vatican II, using the symbol of "the People of God," helped usher in a new era for the laity. While this did not lead to "lay trusteeism" or the end of "corporation sole," issues and polities from the past to which we have referred, it did very much mean an enlarged role for the laity. Most Catholic colleges and universities declericalized and semisecularized, turning to laity for leadership. Whenever the Vatican tried to exercise measures that would restrict the freedom of academic pursuit or to affect hiring policies, these lay leaders did what they could to remain loyal to Catholic intention but to press for higher academic excellence. Lay people often edited the diocesan and other newspapers. Yet some laity also saw Vatican II as license for "anything goes."

The curia in Rome and some American bishops did not learn the fundamental point that John XXIII seemed to know by instinct and Paul VI kept learning or half-learning through bitter experience. In the modern free world, the church must make its way through persuasion, not coercion. Whenever it persuaded the many among the over fifty million faithful—an awesome figure in a free society where neither fear of hell nor societal penalties were available—they willingly followed. Indeed, it was hard to keep them from following. Thus in the matter of opposition to abortion after the *Roe v. Wade* Supreme Court decision of 1972, lay militants chided the hierarchy for not being fanatic on the cause. On the other hand, where the laity was not persuaded, they could not easily be coerced. Thus on a kin issue, as we shall later see in a larger context, "artificial birth control," the polls showed well over 80 percent of Catholic couples employing condemned means in good conscience. They could not be coerced. When the Vatican took coercive means, as when it chastised and wanted to expel members who pointed to Catholic pluralism on abortion and other issues, it had to be content with purging religious orders and disciplining priests. The laity had become harder to reach.

Sexuality was another dimension of change. The hearty regard for conjugality and genital expression within marriage

185

that characterized the Hebrew scriptures was tempered somewhat by the ascetic preoccupations of Jesus and Paul and the early church. For reasons too complex to detail here, not all of them well understood, the Catholic church through the ages put high premiums on virginity, chastity, and celibacy. The sexual act even in marriage was therefore often viewed negatively. Catholic leadership at and after the Council saw to a transvaluing here. The church spoke even more warmly of conjugality and marital sexuality. These affirmations were another easily corruptible element in reform. An "anything goes" emphasis began to appear here and there. Some promoted a kind of Catholic acceptance of what was called "New Morality" and other features of the sexual revolution. The Bad New Days people have no difficulty finding references from those who were extreme in their advocacies. Such critics therefore overlooked some genuine Catholic gains in respect to recovery of the richer biblical approaches to sexuality.

Still another area of delicate and easily upset balance had to do with freedom in the church. All but a few radical Catholics knew that freedom in society and freedom in the church had somewhat different norms. Any organization, whether or not it makes supernatural claims for its norms, has a right to set some reasonable guidelines and boundaries and try to enforce them. Thus, for example, it may be legally legitimate to divorce in society on grounds that the church may find unacceptable and may condemn. When the clash between value systems is too great, the church may find it difficult to compel loyalty. It may have to do some adjusting or it may lose the members who do not find the norms plausible. Catholic academic freedom in theology is not so vast that one can teach *any* manifest heresy under the sun and label it Catholic orthodoxy. One cannot do everything with the canons of the church and claim license for this because nothing in civil law prevents such exercises. All that is understood.

What was less easy to work with was the question of where and how to draw the lines after Vatican II. The mourners about the Bad New Days would draw the lines tight and high and hard. They would have bishops enforce the rules as they, the critics, see them. Thus in 1968 when Pope Paul VI issued *Humanae Vitae*, against birth control, theologians led by Charles Curran at Catholic University of America dissented. Several hundred professors made their dissent public. There were even demonstrations in support of academic freedom. The critics thought there was nothing to argue about, which was precisely the point at issue, because "Rome had spoken."

What was overlooked was that the critics themselves were often selective about what they wanted to hear from Rome and where they wanted to disagree. The dissenters, meanwhile, wanted to keep the debates alive. In the specific case of *Humanae Vitae*, they knew that the majority of the pope's own chosen counselors, experts in biblical or theological studies and married couples themselves, had advocated some changes. Pope Paul, not heeding them, seemed to argue less on the basis of biblical and theological norms and more on the notion that to make a change would call into question the teaching authority of the church. He would be departing from what his immediate predecessors had pronounced as the truth, and that could lead to a crisis of faith. Sociologist Andrew Greeley, after extensive surveys, found that just the opposite was the case. Because they claimed to find the reasoning faulty, the interpretation of marital experience misguided, the theology partial and weak, the injunction and enforcements arbitrary, many Catholic couples were led to a crisis of faith and confidence by the pope and *Humanae Vitae*. Nothing had done more since the Council, argued Greeley, to upset things than had this papal action.

187

A fifth area was liturgical. During the year after the Council new regulations went into effect. The Mass was to be said in the vernacular, with the priest facing the people. The mystery was not to be conjured through arcane actions almost out of sight at the end of a chancel. The mystery was now located with the presence of Christ in the midst of the gathered People of God. The greeting or Kiss of Peace was restored after long neglect. The faithful could receive the cup of wine along with the host, and the host could now be recognized as bread, real bread, and not an ill-defined plastic-looking wafer. Private confession was still expected and encouraged, but the norm would now be confession in community before the Eucharist. There was henceforth less premium on saying the rosary or attending novenas and benedictions. Self-discipline, not church law, was called upon for the teaching of restraint. This meant, most vividly, that Catholics could eat meat on Fridays and in Lent. There were accompanying new rules for mixed marriages and the ceremonies attendant to weddings. A Protestant minister, for example, could often share in the rite. Catholics could attend non-Catholic worship. There was formal proscription against but practical ambiguity about communion with non-Catholics, but certainly the old legalism had gone.

These changes are so familiar now that only the senior generation can recall the liberation and the subsequent trauma for many. Those who liked the Good Old Days rallied around people like Father Gomar DePauw. He more or less bootlegged Latin masses for the nostalgic or for the legalists who rejected the whole Vatican Council II out of hand, and, in Catholic terms, "illegally." At the other extreme some had trouble finding self-discipline. They engaged in heady expressions of liberty. There were reports of an underground church that met in high-rise apartments, often priestlessly. The participants held what they called a Eucharist that featured Coke in paper cups and any sort or concept of bread, interpreted as one would. These extravagances were always the exception. They were probably rare, necessarily short-lived. They went out of vogue as quickly as they came into fashion. Most Catholics, after the sampling, took the aspects of the new that they found attractive. Then, under episcopal and liturgical commissioners' guidance, they came up with a more conservative compromise. Literary purists had much to complain about in the translations and the style of new prayers. It takes decades, perhaps centuries, to develop classic liturgical speech. Musical purists rued the replacement of the organ by thrumming, numbing guitars. They regretted the absence of an appropriate hymnody. Yet the surveys, even at a time in the mid-eighties, showed that the clear majority of those at Eucharist welcomed the new communicative forms. They complained, as had their grandparents, about the low quality of many of the homilies. That is, as is the case of other threatening topics, we are happy to say, a theme for another day, another place.

I have used these five changes as samples to discern a kind of "Anatomy of Revolution" in Catholicism. First there is control, restraint, to the point of absurdity. Then there is pressure against the restraints, voiced in a time of discontent and new ferment. In Catholicism, that movement was the eve of the Second Vatican Council, or, in our terms, the Weigel-Murray era. Third is controlled adaptation to change, as in the Council decrees. This is followed by experiment. Now occurs conflict between those who would push the new freedoms to extremes and those who resisted change all along. Most priests, religious, and laity moved now here, now there, but seldom to extremes. A fifth stage sees a kind of synthesis that cannot satisfy these extremes, but that permits the church to move ahead and focus on other agenda items.

Power

Such items were not lacking after the Council. We have already mentioned Dorothy Day's pioneering in the Catholic Worker Movement. She put her resources to work and her name and body on the line in movements as remote as support of La Causa. This was a largely Hispanic movement under Cesar Chavez, a cause that welcomed clerical and religious support. Its rites often centered in the Catholic Mass. It would organize farm workers into unions that, leaders argued, would offer more justice than the non-union or old union approaches did.

To names like hers were added those of the brothers Daniel and Philip Berrigan, priests and social radicals. Poet Daniel stayed in his religious order and combined deep devotionalism and literary aspiration with a conscience devoted to causes. Philip eventually left his order and married a radical former nun. The two were constant figures in demonstrations against nuclear weapons, for civil rights causes, and the like. The media made "the Berrigan brothers" demonstrator celebrities. Here their names have to stand for women and men of courage and sometimes folly who took personal risks, were often imprisoned, and spoke up on controversial causes. When they departed from what was recognized by others as the Catholic tradition they could be dismissed as relics or clichés, stereotypical agitators who did not reach consciences.

On the other hand, countless more were seen as drawing upon that tradition. The great French Catholic socialist Charles Péguy once contended: "Everything begins in mysticism and ends in politics." Those who acted as if Catholicism had power because it could coerce consent by members forget this source. Those who acted as if they could exploit the interest and the capital their parents had invested in the church soon found it gone. Those who recognized that the church cannot raise armies,

190

extort taxes, or force continued membership had a different approach. They knew that the only power it had came from shared memory and hope, shared belief and prayer. Unless they kept feeding that power source by attentiveness to Catholic resources and expectations, they lost power and dispersed.

That the Catholic social causes were not beside the point in a world threatened by the bomb and a nation with economic injustices came to be clear to the whole nation when in 1983 and 1984 the bishops issued drafts of pastoral letters on nuclear weaponry and peace and then on the economy. That they issued these at all was a sign of maturity in American Catholicism. Some highly visible curial figures in the Vatican did not believe that national councils of bishops should be so independent, so public. Yet the bishops found that they could not keep silence on the most troubling issues of the day, and they spoke up.

The mass media gave so much attention to the content of these letters that a writer serves better in this historical context by pointing to their form, their approach. The same communicators in the media were often naive about the history. They did not seem aware of all the provincial and plenary councils. They overlooked the fact that from 1919 to the years of the pastorals, the NCWC and the *Bishops' Program* had been articulated. They did not know or remember that for many years Monsignor George Higgins was representing the bishops at collective bargaining tables, next to labor leaders like Walter Reuther and management in the auto and other industries. They did not know of the Bishop Bernard Sheils or the Monsignor John Egans and their countless counterparts (if not their matches) in many cities. These were urban "fixers" in the positive sense of the term who worked on issues of poverty, race, and the like. Most press and television coverage was not able to put into perspective the issuing of these episcopal letters.

191

Several elements are remarkable. First, the letters are persuasive, not coercive. They invite dialogue and show the bishops ready to be taught by other Catholics. There is here an awareness of post-World War II laity, more often than not a college-bred laity that can do its own thinking and that must be consulted in its arena of expertise. Second, if it is Catholic, it is also ecumenical. The reaching out that recent popes praised is exemplified. The argument is not "God says . . . The Bible says . . . The church says . . . The pope says . . . so you must follow." Instead, the letters point to certain principles that are binding on Catholics while their applications are complex and ambiguous. Other Christians are invited to take part. Third, they show an awareness of pluralism. They reach out to "people of good will," where these share the same Catholic faith or have other or no recognizable faith at all.

This dialogical style came to prevail. With its own kind of call upon authority, it came to be so accepted that only occasionally were there reminders of the old style. Pope John Paul II himself, an immensely potent figure on the world and American scene, did not always show an awareness of what the bishops were explicating. He knew that in Poland, a divided but less pluralist society, the communist regime gives unity to the church factions. There are not many other strong religious elements with which to deal. Where it is hard to be a Catholic, as in Poland, it is easy to be a Catholic. Where it is easy to be a Catholic, as in America, it is harder to be a Catholic. There are here so many alternatives or lures, and the faithful have to be convinced.

In the 1984 presidential campaign some bishops said or implied that a Catholic could not run for office without making legal proscription of abortion a visible theme. A few even hinted that Catholics might not in conscience be free to vote for such a candidate. There was considerable reaction. Only naive and uninformed Americans, some of them prominent, argued that bishops had no right to express their views in politics. More people questioned whether the implicit endorsement of candidates and the explicit invoking of threats was not a breaking of "the rules of the game." Had the ecumenical spirit not been strong and had Catholic varieties in American politics not been rich and often unyielding, one might have heard more complaint that such bishops were demonstrating the legitimacy of the fears of anti-Catholics in Nativist periods. Some curial officials in 1984 condemned without a hearing the religious and priests who signed an advertisement that merely pointed to Catholic diversity in respect to abortion and called for dialogue over it. The issues then again came to the fore. Murray was right: pluralism in society would not marvelously cease to trouble the human city. He could have added that pluralism in the church would not cease marvelously to trouble Catholicism.

Theology

Theology was one field in which this pluralism had to be evident. Many Catholic theologians had long chafed over their roles. They knew about the promise of the developmental theologies of Johann Adam Möhler and cardinal John Newman in Germany and England in the nineteenth century. Most did concur with the substance of the papal condemnations of Modernism. They also knew, however, that these condemnations had made theologians timid, had dampened their enthusiasm for doing in their day what Augustine and Aquinas had done in their own. They were aware of stirrings in Europe. There Karl Adam led early ecumenical endeavors in Germany. Names like Yves Congar and Henri de Lubac typified French experiment. Not all Americans were content to force all theology any longer into the mode of officially endorsed Thomism. Why not put existentialism, personalism, or process thought to the service of God and church? In 1943 in *Divino Afflante Spiritu*, the pope had recognized moderate forms of biblical scholarship. In Jerusalem and Paris there were honest and faithful biblical critics who were not afraid lest their research lead to a loss of faith. They instead expressed faith in the text and the revelation and wanted to use these to enhance Christian life. They were not permitted to.

The Vatican Council after 1962 honored the new theology when *periti*, experts, came along to Rome with bishops from everywhere. It was instantly apparent that many differing thought forms, worldviews, and philosophies informed theology in the nations, universities, and dioceses of the Catholic world. Figures like Germany's Karl Rahner were recognized as orthodox and probing at once. Rahner opened his theological work with anthropological reference. He argued that the first words one says about God are located in what one can say about the responding subject, the human. Rahner, who did not speak English, was a "boiler room" theologians' theologian. He influenced the men and women who knew that the average member of the American Catholic Church and the public did not understand his transcendental philosophy. Yet by the time of his death in 1984 Rahner was recognized as having had incomparable influence on American Catholic thinkers.

A younger German with rhetorical gifts and charisma, Hans Küng was more attractive to the media and more controversial in the church. His American tours after the Council drew enormous crowds. He spoke of the need for reform and renewal. Küng's themes favored Council and collegiality over papal expression. He spoke in these terms for freedom in the church. He and his Belgian counterpart, Edward Schillebeeckx, explored the roots of ministry. They contended that the decisions about priesthood made in nineteenth-century Catholicism followed defensive authority models. These did not always match the "evangelical" and "charismatic" styles of biblical and early Christianity. They wanted to bring about change. Both men became controversial. The Vatican put restrictions on Küng's scope but could not restrict his thought or influence. It kept a watchful eye on Schillebeeckx. Theologians began to be cautious.

In due course some came to champion various political or liberation theologies. These interpretations of faith began with a single interpretive principle: that the God of the Bible sides with the poor and oppressed. That this God is so often portrayed on that side in the Bible was unquestionable. The idea gave impetus, particularly in Latin America, to movements of reform and sometimes of revolution. These efforts would break the old ties between the church and repressive regimes. There were several problems, however. Some advocates used Marxian analytic tools that were suspect because of old contexts of Marxian atheism. When some moved into Marxist-style prescriptions, beginning with violent class warfare, the issue grew more complex. The fact that socialist revolutions often led to new repression, sometimes against the church, gave the Vatican pause. The additional fact that some priests were drawn into violence further fed the controversy. Less noticed, said partisans, was the way in which in the absence of liberation theology violence and repression were already present. Church people in any case were the prime sufferers. When officials at the Vatican began making charges and inquiries into the thought of prominent liberationists, this was ominous in the eyes of North American champions.

Liberation theology was not the norm in North American seminaries. It had promised or threatened to become so during the revolts of the sixties. That decade, however. revealed that most Americans do not regard themselves to be in pre-revolutionary situations. Marxist analysis may suggest some reasons as to why this is so and why inequities and injustices can be so great. Marxist techniques for change, however, were clearly not welcomed. They would be seen as counterproductive, also in the eyes of many of the theologians. Liberation, then, found its main areas of impact in respect to Latin Americans, sometimes to support black, Hispanic, or other minority causes; often to legitimate the women's revolution in church and society.

Most experimental Catholic thought went to other causes. Theologians like David Tracy, Avery Dulles, Richard McBrien, Elizabeth Schüssler-Fiorenza, Monika Hellwig—what one hazards to mention a few out of a large cast!—showed a sense of faithfulness to the main themes of Catholic tradition. Yet they were interpreters in an age of criticism. They wanted to use "hermeneutics," methods of interpretation that reckon with the preunderstandings text-readers bring to their later understandings. They wanted to be "phenomenological," which meant that they wanted to understand the phenomena of religious experience and expression while bracketing their own presuppositions along the way. This meant that they had to put aside the impulse to be report card graders, constant labelers of orthodoxies, simple enemies of the secular. Their work may not directly have faced the people. Few became celebrities. Yet through seminars, journals, conferences, lectures, and institutes, their ideas were translated to where they had effect on lay people in the congregations.

Women

Mention of professors Schüssler-Fiorenza and Monika Hellwig evokes a host of names, beginning with Rosemary Ruether, and a range of topics connected with a "women's revolution" in the church. Women made up more than half of the Catholic populations for at least two centuries in America. They were excluded from the priesthood, so it was harder for them to get their names in indices of history books. Yet Catholic history has seen so many accomplished members of orders and lay women that they made their mark. This book, for instance, begins with Isabella, moves to the Indians and Tekakwitha, soon finds the first American saint in Elizabeth Seton, and follows saintliness down to Dorothy Day. Yet the theological status of women was usually uncertain. Where certain, it left them in secondary church roles and, until recently, often unsupported in society outside the home and family.

All that was to change in what could turn out to be the most drastic of the post-Vatican II changes. Critics of "the women's movement" radicals wrote off the whole venture as a mere concession to the *Zeitgeist,* the spirit of the times. They thought it was a selling out to secular feminism and faddism. Now, only superficial history would overlook the connections and dependencies. Yet advocates of women's causes and consciousness in the church were not long put off by such charges. Often a secular trigger does set off a Christian charge. The late Hannah Arendt, for instance, liked to show that Christian groups, Catholic and not, vie with each other, each claiming that it had invented democracy or republican constitutionalism. If so, she asked, why did it take 1800 years for Christians to discover this impulse in their treasures? The Enlightenment, secular outlooks, public causes all played their part. If so, she implied, Christians might well first send a card of thanks to the secular order that helped them.

Something like this was the case with women's liberation. In its earliest stages the movement was extreme. This seemed necessary for calling attention to itself and was inevitable as an expression of rage. Yet like all such movements—one thinks of "Black Power!"—the "Sisterhood is beautiful" theme did not often take the form of strident, anti-male, anti-Christian theologies. Its enemies found these easily in the thought of Mary Daly and then tried to imply it was widespread if not universal. Much of the impulse for change instead came from new styles of living that were very common in the Western world and especially in North America. This spoke less directly to or out of the concerns of people in what was called the Third World. American economic necessity or choice, accompanied by a desire for women to find fulfillment also in careers outside the home, led them to combine spousehood and parenthood with professional careers. Others chose to remain single and seek such fulfillment. Along the way many became aware of injustices in respect to women in the wage and market place. At home they no longer would accept status that implied inferiority, not complementarity. In the church. . . .

The women who turned to the church for resource paid it a compliment. They knew that for all the grandeur in biblical understandings of women, there were also statements that reflected the very different cultures of past days. They also became convinced that Roman Catholic limits on sacramental ministry were not integral to the biblical witness and did not square with other elements of Catholic tradition and modern possibility. Much of the impulse for the ordination of women came from North America, where many Catholic seminaries welcomed great numbers of women who were in curricula designed for priestly ministry. There was not much chance that during the rule of Pope John Paul II there would be license for them to be ordained. Yet they hoped against hope and worked for change while preparing themselves. They were careful, however, not to make ordination to priesthood the whole cause, since it directly affected only a minority. Justice, rights, dignity, fulfillment for all women were the more common themes.

Spirituality   The post-Vatican II church has been more than an agency for social change. The arguments about its place in public life are meeting points with the larger society, but they appear only periodically as episodes. They attract mass communicators and historians more than the people who make up the body of the faithful. For every Dorothy Day Worker's House there are a million Catholic households. For every Hans Küng arguing theology there are a million less literate sayers of prayers. For every pair of Berrigans demonstrating for causes there are thousands of pairs of unnamed and unknown battlers for quiet victories. They work to overcome their own alcoholism or alienation. They care about the upbringing of children and the rites of the dying. While the theologians move into exciting and urgent aspects of medical ethics, they simply want to know how to be well and whole. They call upon God and church to be of help. They do not seek out social causes far from home. Yet many are also attentive to these. They care about the whole world and church but they necessarily concentrate on care of the aged, countering a drug culture, and assuring medical care where they live. The Catholic story and the churchly body make history in these respects, too; and this story dare not end without notice of them.

Spiritual styles do change; they have a history. After the agitations of the 1960s, as if in reaction, society quieted. Church people also directed energies to hitherto partially neglected aspects of life. Words that came to characterize many of the ventures were "the spiritual journey" or "the inner life." During the periods of institution building in the fifties and the upheavals of the sixties, people still prayed as before. Books on positive thinking, self-help, and spiritual benefit never went wholly out of style. Bookstore managers for a time noticed that the old devotional literature did not hold attention. Spiritual retreats seemed old hat. The contemplative orders had hard times. The movement to the monastery door in the path of people like Thomas Merton was replaced by people being dispensed from vows. They returned from the world of the convent to the temptations of the world's surroundings. A secular style was expected to prevail.

No one foresaw and, at first, not many noticed a change. Somewhere in the later 1960s, however, people turned inward, often necessarily and generously, sometimes selfishly, as if their quest were the purpose of the world's creation. They would connect with other seekers, with the deepest fonts of their own being, with the life in God which was immemorially to be an address of the restless, disquieted heart.

Some of the young, including the Catholic young, carried the restlessness into pathetic quests for a single spiritual fix. This led them to experiment with communal living. They rejected tradition and family and joined what came to be called "cults" from the Orient or the occult worlds. The founding dates of many "new religions" in America are within five years of each other. The public became aware of Krishna Consciousness, the Unification Church, the Divine Light Mission, Nichiren Shoshu, Transcendental Meditation, and any number of other advertised and recruiting options. Many of these bred ephemeral attachments. The experimenters left radicalism and cultism behind and settled back to adulthood in the world of computers and jogging. Others stayed with the serious aspects of Eastern thought. The day he died in 1968, Thomas Merton had been in Southeast Asia, lecturing to Buddhist and Hindu monks from whom he had learned. Jesuits in Japan absorbed something of Zen ways of thinking and exported them to America. Many of the Oriental emphases lived on in therapies, holistic health causes, and library study.

Other new expressions became institutionalized and popular. The best known example of these is Catholic Pentecostalism or the charismatic movement. In biblical Christianity there were some who "spoke in tongues" and interpreted such tongue speaking. They prophesied and healed. Throughout Catholic history small movements of ecstatics and enthusiasts, mystics and healers, kept something of this tradition alive. Many expected it to disappear on modern soil, which was too sterile to encourage meditation, mysticism, mystery, magic, metaphysics, or almost anything else spiritual that started with "m." People turned out to be surprising. They were more rich in resources, more eager to find meaning and less eager merely to function.

On Protestant soil, where Methodism, "perfectionism" and "holiness movements" started the motion late in the nineteenth century, there was an eruption around 1900 in Kansas and 1906 in Los Angeles and then all through the southeast. Women and men, black and white, merged in a common but varied movement. They claimed that they could reclaim the tongue-speaking and other "gifts of the Spirit" of the first Pentecost. They were called Pentecostal. Through the decades, scores of white and black denominations and movements developed. Their members tended to be seen as back-country, low-caste, hillbilly, holy-roller types, hardly attractive to middle-class mainstream people or religious groups.

Then in a conventional Episcopal church in Van Nuys, California, in 1960 the priest and some members began speaking in tongues. Soon the movement spread elsewhere in Episcopalianism, Lutheranism, Methodism, and in other denominations that did not encourage *glossolalia,* as it was called, or the concept of a second baptism, a Spirit-baptism, in their traditions. In an ecumenical age such a movement was not stoppable short of Roman Catholicism.

In 1967 at Duquesne in Pittsburgh and then at Notre Dame and the University of Michigan soon after, "tongues" broke out, as they say. Groups and then communities formed. They sought patrons. Some theologians like Killian McDonnell and Donald Gelpi soon favored them. Cardinal Leon Joseph Suenens encouraged charismatics from distant Belgium and during American tours. Father and later Mr. Francis McNutt became a popular healer. *As the Spirit Moves* was but one of many book titles.

All this charisma gets routinized, say the sociologists. Spontaneous eruptions turn ordered. The charismatic movement acquired expectable forms. There were huge summer rallies at Notre Dame and Kansas City. Enduring communities formed, as at Ann Arbor, Michigan. They usually developed what to outsiders looked like an authoritarian male-dominated cast, even if more women were participants than men. Publishing houses and periodicals were formed or oriented to meet the new market. Manuals told how to hold prayer meetings on Thursday nights. There were metropolitan gatherings of charismatics who waved their arms in the air, moved rhythmically, and chanted or spoke in syllables that need not connect intelligibly. They would be open to the Spirit. Sometimes they connected with Protestant Pentecostals and picked up elements of biblical fundamentalism from them. Others were more liberal, eager to put their new mysticism to political use, as Péguy would have it. They were a distinct minority.

Such actions inspire reactions. The pope and the bishops were careful to show interest but not to condemn them, only to warn against extravagances. The Catholic Pentecostals were often welcomed for their spiritual gifts where these were advertised as great boons to be added to Catholicism. They were often cautioned against or despised when the charismatics acted as if *not* to have their gifts made one less than a full Catholic Christian.

In the early days of the movement, the charismatics often spoke as if we were entering the Third Age, the age of the Spirit, as prophesied almost a thousand years ago by Joachim de Fiore. This unquenchable fire would spread everywhere. Yet, like so many movements, it crested after fifteen years. There were divisions in the ranks. Some wanted to move their spiritual styles into the conventional parish devotional lines, at the risk of being merged back among all other renewal groups. Others wanted to push their spiritual styles into unconventional directions to test the tolerance of other Catholics, especially the leadership. This would give them clear identity, mission, and purpose, but would risk schism.

Through the years, charismatics learned to live with the rest of the church, and much of the rest of the church learned to live with them. It became clear that they would not sweep the field. Too many fully orthodox and deeply spiritual Catholics were not, by personality or character or in their theological search, attracted. Pentecostalism would have to settle for being part of the church, never anything like the sweeping whole. It will share its place among other Catholic innovations and carryovers at the end of the century, in a very different world than the one we call "post-Vatican II." The Soviet Union, the Communist rival to America, Catholicism, and American Catholicism, imploded in 1989. The tensions between the tribes and peoples on so many continents also ended. The church internationally and domestically is now in a very different situation. We are still post-Vatican II, but in the final chapter there is another "post-" to plant, and to it we turn.

Postmodernity: 1985-

Namings   This postscript on postmodernism gives us a chance to look at the present and point to the future. Catholicism these years is beginning its sixth century since it became part of the world that many called New in the hemisphere they named Western. Catholicism is also expectant about life in the third millennium after Christ. What is its postmodern circumstance?

Postmodern: the term is distasteful to some, who wonder why so many things have to be called "post-" these years. Why not wait until an age has its own name instead of labeling it with a tag from another epoch? Why name it at all? How can we be sure that a new era is upon us? Is not the act of naming a sign of boredom with things as they have been and are, an impulse of "with it" people to be the first to stake a claim on a new temporal territory, a fashion of faddists who will in their own old age already be embarrassed as their successors look back on a time that did not yet need a "post-" to describe it, a time that had too much in common with what went before, elements that those of us who necessarily yet lack perspective cannot have seen?

The three question marks in that paragraph can serve as caution signs, but they cannot creatively serve as inhibitors or barriers as we set out in one more effort to understand the story of American Catholicism. Whether or not the name postmodern survives or should survive, it can serve as a signal of change, a symbol of restlessness, an urge to make sense of things. Since postmodern can mean many things to different people— admitting *that* is a sign that postmodernity is here, some would say—it is in order for me to say how it is being conceived and here used. Postmodern presupposes modern.

Scholars conventionally divide the story of Christianity into ancient, medieval, and modern chunks. Some with finesse insert reformation between medieval and modern, but they would not do that had not Protestants read the story of the sixteenth-century reformation as their Book of Genesis, their beginning. They did so with sufficient success that Catholics had to start talking about the Counter-reformation or, better, the Catholic reformation, because there *was* one concurrent with and partly independent of the storms stirred by people named Luther, Calvin, Zwingli, Knox, and the rest. The Catholic reformation was one of the impulses that was current with and that inspired the voyages of exploration, the settlement, the conquests and missions of the sixteenth century.

Ancients did not wake up talking about living in the ancient world. Those who inhabited the Middle Ages leave not a trace of a clue that they were living in the middle ages, between what before—and what after? But moderns were more impatient and started naming their epoch and its styles, thus carrying the virus that impels talk about postmodernity today.

What are some of the characteristics of modernity? It was and, selectively, is a period colored by cosmopolitan, internationalist impulses. One can get a notion from looking at a visible symbol of modernity, the modern skyscraper style in architecture. Skyscrapers in this model aspire to be rational, linear, unadorned, capable of being anywhere, showing no trace of roots or emplacement. An embassy in New Delhi could as well have been placed in London or Nairobi. The skylines of Hong Kong, Chicago, Buenos Aires, or Johannesburg, at least from a distance, look similar. Closer up one can see that the postmodernists are violating the international style and coming up with eclectic experiments, but they have not yet won.

Spiritually, this international style was to be marked by the rationality and the scientific spirit of the eighteenth-century Enlightenment, which depended little or not at all on "m" words like mysticism, mystery, magic, metaphysics, or miracle to explain itself to itself. For two centuries Catholicism, including American Catholicism, was busy accommodating itself to this modern style—or engaging in heroic acts of resistance and defiance. These often made it look crabby rather than innovative and open to the Spirit. In postmodern times, however, it is harder to locate the style that is to be defied or adapted to. The modern secular world is secular from many angles; it "rounds itself off" without reference to anything transcendent or sacred. But just under the surface, people and peoples are back favoring those "m" word things, mixing the secular with the spiritual impulses in new and puzzling ways.

This essay on what one person means by postmodernism will be most clear if we keep in mind the visual version of it, having begun to bring it up by reference to architecture. Not believing in the linear, rational, coherent, and unadorned style, the postmodern architect seems uninhibited and eclectic. She can draw on any past expression, using elements of romanesque, gothic, baroque, or modern styles, jowl of stone by cheek of glass. In sculpture the postmodernist seeks an esthetic experience by assembling autobumpers, arms from Greek statues, mirrors, pieces of wood and fur, or whatever. Words ending in "age" capture the eclectic spirit that finds some coherence in chaos, or some equivalent of beauty in elements of order that do not seem well to coexist. The artist takes bits of canvas, feathers, clippings, photographs, souvenirs, antiquarian items, and shopping lists, and creates what is then called an assembl*age*, a mont*age*, a coll*age*. [Enemies of it all call it garb*age*.]

So with things of the spirit. Apparently contradictory elements live side by side. The postmodern American Catholic scene is rich in paradoxes, full of mismatches that seem to bother few or at least that can be controlled by no one, jarring juxtapositions. We began this book looking for "descript" Catholicism, but seem to be beguiled or benumbed by the nondescript.

The current move of history is beyond pluralism; many describe the United States and American Catholicism today as "multicultural." A pentagon of peoples with hyphens attached to their name seem to have their own preserves and perspectives, to the exclusion of others: Afro-, Asian-, Euro-, Native- and Hispanic-Americans appear to form more separated and intact cultures, whether Catholic or not, than do Catholics, whatever their racial and ethnic lineages. Postmodern Catholicism reckons with gender experience, as masculine, feminine, bisexual, gay, and lesbian parties in the church make claims for the utter distinctiveness of their hold on the Catholic story, usually over against the "ists" or "phobes" who resist the idea of letting them have it to themselves. Social class, ideology, and personal preference alike become the measures of what was or is Catholic inside multiculturalism.

Closer up, the postmodernist sees that multiculturalism is still too coherent a notion to be serviceable. Take the instance, crucial to Catholicism, of what it is to be "Hispanic." A score of millions, and more coming and counting, are now Hispanic, and they are described as having a different Catholicism than the Euro- people brought. Yet how can the Catholic Church, including Hispanics in it, plan strategy if it does look too close? Thus, what do Mexican migrant farmers or urban officeworkers in the Southwest have in common, so far as Catholic style and accent is concerned, with Cubans in Miami, when one brings up religion and politics? And what do these two have in common with the Puerto Rican Catholics in Spanish Harlem? Now and then we hear of a citizen who was Castilian but cannot win the label "Hispanic" in the United States. We are multimulticultural. One has to know of each believer whether such a person is pro-pope or anti; preferring traditional liturgies or new ones or none; being straight or gay; charismatic or near-fundamentalist or Liberationist; on the political right or left; in what way is such a person merely quirky? How to assert authority or seek the common good in a church and movement called Catholic in the face of this? We can now point to several elements in the postmodern mix of change, themes that have become more vivid in the years post- post-Vatican II.

Authority

American Catholics have often shown a liking to Pope John Paul II, as was evidenced by the presence of a couple hundred thousand young people during his visit to Denver in 1993 and in the crowds numbering in the millions in cities during an earlier visit. He is a celebrity, a charismatic figure, a person whose *gravitas*, his grave bearing, holds attention; and he is *theirs*. That is, however much a dissenter one is within the church, however marginal to the Catholic people, one may be, she or he still reckons with the pope. This means that he has to be reckoned with as an authority, as the authority. He makes claims for it and exercises it, whether by standing behind the decision to remove dissenting professor Charles Curran from the Catholic University of America theological faculty in 1986, by promoting a traditional-style universal Catholic Catechism in 1994 or, in the same year, by attacking United States leadership in a United Nations conference on *development*, which he likes, and *population control*, which he mistrusted and despised for promoting contraception and, he claimed, abortion. No mistaking his charism, status, and bid for authority.

Postmodern Catholics, however, are eclectic about when and how to follow this authority. In 1994 the pope came out with as authoritative a statement as possible—or *almost* so, some would say, since he stopped at the brink of calling the teaching "infallible"—against the ordination of women. American Catholic women by the thousands were bidding to be ordained and by the millions favored such a sacred act (though it must be said, congruently with our plot, that the most vehement public support for his prohibition of it also came from conservative Catholic women). With one stroke of a pen he not only said he was forbidding their ordination, but he went on to forbid even talking about the subject in any pattern of advocacy. Forbidding talk is the best way to stimulate talk in a free society and a church that often questions authority, including papal authority. So talk goes on, even when hope has also left. So women who supported ordination of women write essays on "Why I Remain in the church." But many of them remain, questioning authority on one topic and living with it easily on another.

Simple rejection of the sort seen right after Vatican II, when thousands of priests and nuns and lay people left the church in disgust, followed the neat lines of the modern age. A rational line was drawn and you decided on which side of it to be. In post-modern American Catholicism, however, the drawing of lines follows no rational plot; indeed there seems to be little drawing of lines. So, the pope says this on one subject, and I find him compelling and agree with him. Then, says this kind of Catholic, I will go along with him. On another subject, he sounds too capitalist or too socialist, too misogynist or patriarchal; then, goes this reasoning, I will enjoy Catholic peoplehood with him being present, but not as my authority.

American Catholicism, in short, shares a crisis of authority, as it has been outlined by Notre Dame professor Mark Chaves. There are as many jurisdictions, canons, and authorities (elected, appointed, or by automatic status) in the church as ever; these are each regarded as having their appropriate functions. But none of them have authority that is automatically conferred; they have to win it. As sports figures say, "You can't win 'em all," and the pope and other leaders do not do so. Twice in recent years, as we saw in the previous chapter, the American Catholic bishops delivered themselves of reasoned comment: on peace (and against nuclear weaponry) in 1983, and on the economy in 1986. Many of the same Catholics who celebrate Catholic authority in general were eclectic in their responses to these. Few Catholics in the military or defense industry gave evidence of having changed their minds about weaponry and the limits of just war theory because of the episcopal argument, despite the huge publicity given the bishops' statement. The very Catholic political conservatives who make a hero of the pope for his having stood up to the Soviet nemesis that was a spectre over his Poland and who can write a pastoral letter promoting private ownership of property and "capitalist" incentives react negatively when he goes on to blast the culture of consumption and commodification, the very mega-mall culture off which so many Catholics live and which they patronize. Or they attack the bishops for being "socialist" in their letter on the economy. And a third episcopal letter, worked on for ten years, did not even get published as planned in 1993 by a hierarchy that either had too much internal disagreement or who worried too much about internal dissent in the church. Authority then suffered again. Yet, the people write "Why I Remain in the church," and most remain, at least as one of Father Greeley's "communal Catholics," or, in our terms, as members of the Catholic people.

One has to ask what becomes of the descriptness of Catholicism when people with postmodern views of authority vote with their feet, or are eclectic and practical about what to follow in papal teaching, and when to follow it. To ask it further than this, however, threatens to turn this story into a question, and to try to answer it might lead to the preaching of a sermon while violating the friendly outsider status. [It gets ever harder to know who is the outsider, who the insider. The modern ecumenical movement was just that: modern. It had neat, uncluttered lines just like those on the skyscrapers; there was a cosmopolitan style and cast. Today's ecumenism is a crazy-quilt of ad hoc arrangements, criss-crossings of interests and alliances, heavily local and deeply rooted in particulars. So who is the insider, who is the outsider?]

American Catholics have only to be reminded that the problem of authority in postmodern religion is not unique to them. It is only of greatest interest because of the size and power of Catholicism, its history, and both the strenuous claims for it and the elaborate machinery set up to enforce it. If 93% of polled Catholics believe one can reject papal teaching and still be considered faithful, as they say they do, they are talking about "a church becoming a people" precisely in the years when a strong and effective teacher and authority was occupying the papal throne.

Sex

It is impossible to talk of American Catholic eclecticism on the subject of authority without then bringing up the connected issue of sex and gender. And it is impossible to do so precisely because the authorities *do* connect the two and speak up on it so consistently. Non-Catholics who pay no attention to bishops' statements on nuclear armament or the economy are intensely alert to what the church teaches and tries to enforce in the matter of sexual and procreative life. Some of these non-Catholics have crossed all kinds of boundaries that they held to through the modern period, boundaries which held the pope as the antichrist and the church as the whore of Babylon. Suddenly the pontiff and his church became the allies of such Protestant evangelical conservatives because of the natural kinship they feel with the other, their best partners in being "pro-life" and antiabortion.

Postmodern Catholics reveal their new kind of sensibility nowhere more vividly than in the matter of sexual expression and the ethos of procreation. To illustrate: it is clear that in the mind of the pope and the teaching authorities in Rome and among many bishops, the issues of contraception and abortion are twin. Contraception was as vigorously opposed in the papal letter *Humanae Vitae* in 1968 and against a United Nations conference document in 1994 as abortion was opposed in both. They violate Natural Law and God's Law alike, and both interfere with procreative possibilities that have to be governed through other means, namely "natural planning" and sexual restraint.

What the teaching authority brings together, however, the postmodern American Catholic renders asunder. Opinion polls find strong support for churchly opposition to abortion (though less readiness for legal proscription in all cases). In 1978, 47 percent of Catholics (44 percent "voting" the other way) rejected the statement that "the Catholic Church should relax its standards forbidding all abortions under any circumstances." Pose the question in other ways, such as asking whether the Catholic member agrees with the church's opposition to abortion, and the percentage will run much higher. But, whatever Dr. George Gallup and other pollsters find on that issue, on the connected one of contraception, Father Andrew Greeley and other surveyors find that eight or nine out of ten Catholic women simply disagree with, ignore, or openly oppose the official teaching. Clearly, they choose and they pick, they make collages and montages out of authoritative teachings, their experience, their own thinking.

A third illustration: attitudes to divorce, remarriage, and churchly acceptance of the practices. Admittedly, lay Catholics were long confused by what they saw to be arbitrary and favoritistic ways around this one through annulment procedures. But in recent decades they have explicitly disagreed with official teaching and authority on the subject. As early as 1978 by a three to one (69 percent to 23 percent) ratio, they agreed with the statement that "Divorced Catholics should be allowed to remarry in the church." The question of how to justify rejection of this authoritative teaching while holding to others *and* being loyal to the church would have been a stumper within the coherence of modern Catholicism, but goes almost unnoticed in the postmodern version.

214

Fourth, premarital sex. Almost nowhere have there been steeper, more sudden declines in simple acceptance of churchly authority in teaching and practice than here. In 1963 in one survey, 88 percent in a Catholic school study, and six years later, in a broader-based poll by Catholics, it was found that 72 percent said it was always morally wrong. Sixteen years later, in 1986, without a hint of openness to official change in the teaching, only 2 percent of the Catholics were still in the "always wrong" camp. Protestants moved more slowly; in 1969 fewer were ready to say it was always morally wrong; in 1985 more Protestants than Catholics saw wrong in such premarital expression.

Over all, near the century's end, one could still count on Catholics to uphold "the traditional family," "family values," and marital fidelity if not premarital chastity; also, to oppose abortion on principle and for most reasons. But one could not count on them to do this upholding simply because the magisterium of the church taught it and the pope insisted on it. They decided on the basis of their experience as it checked out with churchly teaching. Again, they did so while, as Greeley kept finding and saying, "They like being Catholic. . . ."

Greeley found this affirmation striking in the 1990s because of so many changes since the 1960s. There was no change in the proportion of born Catholics who stopped considering themselves Catholic: only one out of seven. There were not more mixed marriages than before: one out of five then and now were in such marriages. One out of four did say he or she took less pleasure in Catholic commitment when and because some thinkers in the church were being persecuted, but they stayed anyhow. Significantly, Greeley found that they had moved so far beyond being shaped by churchly sexual teaching that only about six percent thought seriously of leaving the church because that teaching disturbed them. In 1968, *Humanae Vitae* had led to great disturbance; by the 1990s, Catholics had figured out ways to remain in the church, to be a part of the community of Catholic people, but to make a pastiche of "approvals" and "disapprovals" on the sexual front.

Laity

Those who worry about the loss of authority, feel strong kinship in Christ with the Catholic church, see the eucharist as the central focus of Catholicism, admire priesthood and see values in celibacy, as this writer does, and sometimes write doleful stories about the decline in the numbers of priests and religious. Their books end on downers, it is said, and they share the spirit of lost morale, malaise, cynicism, hopelessness, and even despair that afflicts many idealists in the church.

There are good reasons to be mournful about the decline in the number of priests, those who celebrate mass, are central to the sacramental life (which is central to the church), and have many professional functions that match so well their preparation and professional ways. The non-Catholic is even free to express dissent against the papal opposition to even considering two instruments that might begin to help relieve the priest shortage in a decade or two: the ordination of women, out of bounds for Catholic discussants, and optional celibacy, for which there is churchly precedent and present practice—oppose the ordination of women in Anglicanism and you can quite likely be accepted, though not celibate, in Roman Catholic priesthood—which is not out of bounds though presently not licit. There are no reasons to bring up the easily available statistics about this change, this decline.

Similarly, one can mourn the blow to the clergy in the nineties, when Protestant and Catholic alike but for the moment

Catholic priests and religious, through sexual scandal, harassment, and even criminal activity produce regular front-page news. Mourning, not outrage, was the expression of Catholic and non-Catholic alike when in 1990 an archbishop had to be removed because of adultery, or the charismatic head of Covenant House was revealed to have sexually exploited boys. These were stories that followed shocking tales of individually tragic and statistically significant immoral and criminal abuse activities. These stories, not always fairly reported, when fairly reported became one of the few new "big news" items to be entered into the Catholic record in the 1990s. Reporting it can contribute to "ending on a downer."

However, the story of a people that "like being Catholic" and choose to identify themselves as such, as one-fourth of Americans do, can hardly be expected to see "Finis" written because of decline in the number of clergy or increase in scandal among them. There have been compensatory factors that allow for an if not happy, at least mixed and often promising ending for the story so far. I refer especially to the "lay revolution," which does not mean a revolt against the church but a drastic change in self-concept and innovation. These factors stimulating lay creativity may have become present because of the travail and trauma in the clergy, but they are not all merely compensatory. Thanks to the Second Vatican Council teaching, the post-World War II GI Bill and mass higher education that attracted Catholics more than anyone else; thanks, further, to hierarchs and priests and theologians who persistently advocated the employment of lay imagination and action, and thanks also to some of the better features of the spirit of the times, the spirit of freedom and foresight, there have been very promising moves by lay women and men not merely to supplement priestly activities but to find new roles.

Postmodern Catholicism is in the bewildering and paradox-ical situation, in the eyes of many non-Catholics and many of the faithful, of seeing women barred from priesthood yet teaching priests-to-be in almost every seminary; moving to the front ranks as Catholic lay people (or, sometimes, religious women) in the teaching of religion and theology in Catholic schools; becoming heads of the Catholic Theological Society and the biblical scholarship groups, and more. Closer to the local parish—which also paradoxically, in postmodern times, after cosmopolitanism was supposed to have won out, is the scene of so much intense action by the Catholic people—one sees a similar enlargement of roles. Women and lay men are pastoral assistants, teaching associates, liturgical ministers, parish and diocesan administrators, doing better than many of the ordained did as they fulfill once-clerical roles.

The postmodern visitor to the postmodern parish has to scratch her head as one sees the ease with which these changing roles have become present in so many dioceses. The Vatican appoints many bishops who are supposed to limit or rule against such expressions, to hold the line, or to be grudging about extension of pastoral and at-the-edge-of-sacramental activities by laity. Yet the phenomena grow and win approval. One fairly typical and by no means irreverent pastoral assistant, as her personal card identified her, had a real sense of both gravity and celebration in respect to the eucharist, the pope and bishops and priests, and the faithful. Yet she did so many things that when I asked her what the few, mainly aged, imported clergy—this was in a growing population and church culture—did, she answered, "They go around blessing the bread Saturday afternoons." Such a sentence will not make it into canon law, books of orders, or diocesan guidelines, but this lay person's set of practices exists responsibly, it would seem, as part of the montage, the assemblage of elements in postmodern Catholicism.

That illustration may be too clerical itself. The lay participation exists far beyond the sanctuary and the parish hall, and is giving a new presence and tone to American Catholicism. The numbers of Catholic leaders in politics has long been of proverbially large size in American life; but today the Catholic presence is felt in ever more and diverse roles and ways. Students of volunteering and voluntary organizational life find that the majority of American adults, even in a time when women—historic volunteer corps that they made up—add work outside the home to the work inside it, and *still* find time to volunteer. These same students find that the majority of consistent volunteers credit their religious outlook as a prime motivator. And the really, really long-term ones tend to participate because they tell a common story and they are part of a common story.

That common story, as depicted on these pages, was once more common than it is today. There was less ethnic diversity, less lay participation in the custodianship of the lore. There was more enforceable authority and thus more coherence, even forced uniformity. Both the juridical and teaching authority of the church and the impulse of the moderns produced measures of consistency and predictability that are hard to recover, or even to conceive of, near the century's end. While one might have looked for more sense of responsibility, the growth in the sense of rights and freedom has allowed for more freedom of expression, more ways to tell and live the story. In a time of multiculturalism one regrets to hear the word poet Carl Sandburg thought the ugliest in the language, "exclusive," used by groups. Exclusivism too often colors the separate stories of Catholic subgroups: men and women, straight and gay, Hispanic and Anglo, Vaticanist and dissenting. The preacher of a sermon based on this story could at least wish that these groups engaged more in mutual (and thus *Catholic*) enrichment and not in mutual distancing and protecting of one's own part of the story.

The story does not need a sermon, however. The ancient, medieval, and modern churches had distinctive challenges, some of which they failed to meet or met disastrously and so many of which they did meet that not only did the church survive but it gave life to its culture, shape to its epoch, and meaning to the lives of its faithful. Whatever the epoch and its collage of styles that is taking shape at the end of the century turns out to be called, and however perilous the trajectory through the tribalism, weapon-filled, and cynical world surrounding and afflicting the church Catholic, there are likely to be future chapters about American Catholic people to write. If Catholicism is marked by imagination, as some of its theologians contend it is; if its sacramental outlook mandates and allows for loving looks at a broken world; if the stories of an apparently nondescript set of individuals and peoples keeps finding enough elements that it can let them be descript, we can expect lively and life-giving stories tomorrow. Someone will then come along and write *A Long History of American Catholicism*.

Prospects   Catholicism has been a presence in the New World for almost exactly half a millennium. Christianity has lived about one-fourth of its life having members in North America. Up to this time, the North American Catholics have not yet produced many pages for the anthologies of Catholic theology or spirituality. They are still often regarded as suspect by popes and other leaders who are suspicious of free life in the midst of pluralism. They also win respect by popes for remaining faithful and growing in such climates. The American church has the reputation of being a "doing" church.

American Catholics may be dismissed by some Christians in the southern world, the home of the new Christian minority, for being from the northern. This means that they live in the rich world, which is often seen as and is the exploiter of the poor. Many economic and military policies of United States Catholics may be seen as part of the problem, not the solution, of social change. The voices from these poor worlds are reminders to and judges of United States Catholicism.

At the same time, thoughtful people around the world know that American Catholics are ever more alert to their contexts and needs. American parishes connect with, support, and learn from or speak for Central and Latin American Catholics. Nuns from the United States are all over the world, in nursing, teaching, showing works of love.

The Christian Church continues to shrink in the northern world as it burgeons in the southern. Losses in Europe are the main cause, since North American Catholicism at least grows with the population. Yet no one is complacent. Religious institutions do not have it easy. What sociologists call "privatism" and what I heard a Cicero, Illinois, "ethnic" Catholic coin as *a la carte Catholicism* has been emerging. People live in high-rises and take long weekend excursions. They are less likely to take responsibility for parish and community than did the families bringing up children in suburban parishes. People marry later, divorce more readily, live singly, retire sooner, have fewer children and have them later; women work outside the home and have fewer hours for volunteer work in churches. There are ever more commercial and entertainment distractions. One could list dozens of reasons apart from "the Death of God," which was seldom mentioned in America a few years after

221

premature or mislabeling reports, to explain why religious institutions are and will remain in trouble.

One of the demonstrable zones in which falling away has occurred is among the young. Once upon a time the adventurous or distracted young wandered and then, when childrearing time came, returned to mass and parish life. It is not clear whether a generation after Vatican II such return will so consistently occur. It may be that the church which five centuries ago pursued western horizons and a century ago still chased the western frontier, may here be locating a new zone for adventure, evangelizing, and attraction to service. This could be among the high-rise dwellers, the young and old who live very private, often competitive, not always spiritually dedicated lives. Maybe some "bands" like those of the Redemptorists will form. Perhaps some new Paulists, or the old ones, for that matter, may rise to find ways to lure and serve such millions.

If so, they will take their place in a long train of discoverers, explorers, settlers, builders, and experimenters who went ahead of them, in the name no longer of the flag of Castile but of the Cross that was on it. They may use vastly different languages than did their predecessors. They might be embarrassed by some of the precedents and pioneers. Yet a careful revisiting of the details of that history shows that not all the sweat and blood was given in futile or self-seeking causes. Not all obedience was legalistic, nor all discipline repressive. Instead, in the lives of people who are both very much like their heirs and very much different, often because of nothing more than the passing of time and changing of circumstance, are signs of faithfulness.

The modern, secular, pluralist world is one in which meanings become confused, reasons get diffused. The faithful are the people who have decided, on balance, that the reasons for thinking and saying "Yes" to the call of God through the church are stronger than the reasons for thinking "Maybe" or saying "No." The people who give voice to such positive responses are the best guarantee that a chapter seven in books like this need not, will not, be the last. They may gain confidence and draw models from some of those who left their mark on the pages and the years that went before. Would it be too quaint to picture them going forth as did the first of their lot, Columbus, five hundred years ago?

Jesus et Maria   Jesus and Mary
Sint nobis in via   Be with us on the way.

Index

225

Modernism, 127, 140–142, 172, 193
Mohler, Johann Adam, 193
Montaigne, Michel de, 57–58
Moors, *see* Islam
Morgan, Edmund, 103
Morison, Samuel Eliot, 35
Mormons, *see* Church of Jesus Christ
    of Latter-day Saints
Morse, Samuel F. B., 130
Muhammad, 25, 26
Muldoon, Bishop Peter J., 153
Multiculturalism, 208–209, 219
Mundelein, Cardinal George
    William, 163–165
Murray, John Courtney, 83, 85, 90,
    174, 178–180, 181, 189, 193
Muslims, *see* Islam

Narvaez, Panfilo de, 31, 33
National Catholic Educational
    Association, 134
National Catholic War Council, (NCWC),
    153–154. *See also* National
    Catholic Welfare Council
National Catholic Welfare Council,
    (NCWC), 153–157, 163, 191. *See
    also* National Catholic War Council
National Union for Social Justice, 162
Native Americans, 14, 15, 22, 29–46;
    passim, 49, 51, 52–55, 56–62;
    passim, 63, 103, 106, 111, 177
Nazism, 162, 163, 164
Neale, Leonard, 87
Nerinckx, Charles, 98–99
Neumann, Saint John, Nepomucene,
    101–102, 103
New Christians, 27–28, 37
New Deal, 156, 163
New England, 50
New France, 50, 52, 56, 58, 63, 64
New Spain, 50, 52, 64
New York Review, 142
Newman, Cardinal John, 193
1960 election, 76, 180–181
1984 election campaign, 192–193
Nineteenth Amendment, 155
Noble Savage, 29–30, 57–58
North American martyrs, 34

Oblate Sisters, 101
Onate, Don Juan de, 45
Optional celibacy, 216
Ordination of women, 210, 216
Organized labor, 137–139, 146, 190
Our Lady of Fatima, 168

Pacelli, Cardinal Eugenio, *see*
    Pius XII, Pope
Papal infallibility, 118, 159, 212–213
Parkman, Francis, 56
Parochial schools, 133–136, 152
Pascendi Dominici Gregis (Pius X), 142
Paul VI, Pope, 102, 103, 182–183, 185,
    187
Paulists, 127, 128, 136, 151, 222
Paul James Francis, Father, 128–129
Peale, Norman Vincent, 180–181
Peguy, Charles, 190, 202
Penal Age, 71–72, 73
Penn, William, 66
Pentacostalism, 200–203
Philip II, King of Spain, 42
Pierce v. Society of the Sisters 158
*Pilgrims in Their Own Land: 500 Years
    of Religion in America* (Martin E.
    Marty), 7
Pius II, Pope, 20
Pius VI, Pope, 87
Pius VII, Pope, 97
Pius IX, Pope, 118, 126
Pius X, Pope, 142
Pius XII, Pope, 166–167, 193
Plenary Councils, 119, 191;
    First, 111, 112; Third, 134
Point, Nicholas, 105
Populism, 157
Populist party, 157
Postmodern Catholicism, *see*
    Catholicism, Postmodern
Postmodernism, *see also* Modernism
Powderly, Terence, 138
Premarital sex, 215
Priesthood, decline of, 216–217
"Privatism," 221
Procreation, ethos of, 213–216
Protestant, The, 108
Protestant-Catholic-Jew (Herberg), 169

229